'This long-overdue book will be an ...ncing knowledge and appreciation of the intricacies c... ...al negotiations at UN headquarters on diverse social, economic and environmental issues, molding disparate interests and subjective agendas into lasting legislative outcomes whose main objectives are to enhance peace and prosperity in harmony with our environment, respect of human rights and women empowerment.'

—Munyaradzi Chenje, Deputy Chief Officer, Secretariat of the Multilateral Fund for the Implementation of the Montreal Protocol; former UN Environment Programme New York Office Deputy Director and Head of Policy Coordination and Inter-Agency Affairs

'It is not enough to eloquently establish positions and red-lines in multilateral negotiations; perhaps it is not even enough to strive to build consensus. Instead, it takes courage, vision and skills to be successful and give meaning to a negotiated outcome, and with their years of experience and involvement in varied multilateral negotiations, Rebecca, Jimena and Ye-Min provide that connection and insight in their book. This is an inventive and resourceful blueprint for any Diplomat or Advisor contemplating a stint with the foremost international organization, the United Nations Organisation.'

—Damptey Bediako Asare, Director of Policy Planning, Monitoring and Evaluation Bureau; Ministry of Foreign Affairs and Regional Integration of Ghana; Former Negotiator for G77 &China, New York

'This is the type of publication I wish I had at the beginning of my UN journey. However, it also provides much needed lessons for seasoned diplomats as well. The messages, insights, and examples, offer that rare glimpse of the inner workings of the UN multilateral process, while also shedding light on the important, and often thankless, role of a country's representative to the UN. It could very well become required reading for future UN diplomats.'

—Carlisle Richardson, former Ambassador of St Kitts and Nevis to the UN; Former Economic Affairs Officer of the UN; author of 'Island Journeys: The Impact of the Island Way of Life at Home and Abroad'

'Jimena, Rebecca, and Ye-Min have done a remarkable job in connecting the theory of negotiation with how it is practiced within the UN. The three of them were amazing colleagues, interlocutors, confidants and versatile negotiators during our collective journey towards Rio+20, the Conference that paved the way for the Sustainable Development Goals, demonstrating what is possible when Governments, the UN bureaucracy, and stakeholders work together.'

—*Farrukh Khan, former G77 negotiator from Pakistan*

'For some, outcomes negotiated at the UN - or in other venues - can mean life or death. For everyone, such discussions offer the potential for an improved situation in a better world. When I arrived for my posting at the UN, the negotiating process was like a black box - nothing was precisely what it seemed. This book, which provides essential guidance for a new negotiator, would have been an immense help to me as I began my tour in New York, shortening the time it took to get up to speed with the ins and outs of multilateral negotiations. It also offers insights for complex and contentious negotiations around the world beyond the UN.'

—*Anne Heidi Kvalsøren, Norwegian Special Representative for the peace process in Colombia*

'Profound, insightful, concrete: this book is a must-read guide for anyone entering the highly complex matters of multilateral negotiations, written by three truly inspiring and talented women. With two of them I had the great privilege to spend many hours negotiating – and I share very fond memories of great cooperation, building trust and even friendship while often sitting at the opposite side of the negotiating table. And these are the things that help making the difference on the way towards a better world.'

—*Sandra Ruppen, former Senior Advisor to the Minister of Foreign Affairs of the Principality of Liechtenstein*

'Being able to negotiate well is a critical skill for each of us. In their book, Wu Ye-Min, Rebecca Webber Gaudiosi, and Jimena Leiva-Roche offer UN diplomats – and negotiators everywhere – practical advice on how to effectively navigate the negotiation process. Using real-life examples and well-crafted nuggets of theory, the authors have provided a succinct and useful guide for improving our approach to negotiation in all facets of our lives.'

—*Elizabeth McClintock, Managing Partner, CMPartners, LLC; Adjunct Assistant Professor of International Negotiations, The Fletcher School, Tufts University; Adjunct Lecturer, SAIS, Johns Hopkins University*

'This book, written by negotiators who have been at the frontline of UN negotiations, provides a firsthand perspective of what it means to negotiate at the UN. It vividly conveys the process and dynamics of UN negotiations, and will play a critical role in preparing policy makers and negotiators from around the world who deal with UN issues.'

—*Noel Gonzalez, Director General for Planning and International Development Cooperation Policies, Mexican Agency for International Development Cooperation (AMEXCID)*

'Three experienced UN negotiators offer an insightful, in-depth, and at times humorous study on how UN negotiations work and diplomats behave. From "package deals" to "silence procedures," this book is more than a guide to negotiations; it is a refreshing, solid and much-needed defense of multilateralism for the 21st century.'

—*Paulo Chiarelli, Counsellor, Brazilian diplomat with over 12 years' experience in climate change and sustainable development negotiations*

'I wish to congratulate my former colleagues Jimena, Ye Min and Rebecca for this timely and insightful behind the scenes look at the United Nations and the intergovernmental negotiating process. Despite its flaws, the United Nations remains our best hope for addressing global threats to peace and security, promoting good human rights practices and for advancing the cause of development. The insights and recommendations from these three talented, experienced and skillful diplomats on how to improve the effectiveness, efficiency and impact of this great organization comes at an important juncture in global affairs. More than ever the world needs a strong, effective and renewed United Nations.'

—*Selwin Hart, Ambassador of Barbados to the United States of America and Permanent Representative of Barbados to the Organization of American States, Embassy of Barbados/Permanent Mission of Barbados to the OAS*

'The United Nations is the place where every country comes to do business and solve problems that require collective action. Whether interests clash or align, countries use the UN to build coalitions around shared purpose – more important than ever in this precarious time. Their negotiators are on the front lines, and these authors are masters of that craft. From their diverse perspectives, they provide a front row seat to how multilateral negotiations are won or lost. Long-time practitioners and first-time students will all find this book essential reading.'

—*Elizabeth Cousens, former US Ambassador to ECOSOC and lead U. negotiator on the Sustainable Development Goals, Deputy CEO of the UN Foundation*

'This book is a master-class in the theory and practice of multilateral negotiations. It reminds us of the unique role which the UN can, and must, play in crafting solutions to the most pressing global challenges. I congratulate the authors on a vivid and highly accessible account of the factors which deliver successful UN outcomes. This is essential reading for all who wish to play their part as UN negotiators in fashioning a better world for us all.'

—*David Donoghue, former Permanent Representative of Ireland and co-facilitator of the Intergovernmental Negotiations on the 2030 Agenda*

'Based on their experience of recent years, Ye-Min, Rebecca and Jimena have written this guide on the dynamics of multilateral interactions which shape the decisions of the principal organs at the United Nations. It is meant as a handbook for those that actually participate in the negotiations, reflecting anything from simple statements to formal resolutions and declarations, and showing the wide breadth of activities that go into their work. From the trivial to the momentous, I found it a highly readable and illuminating book.'

—*Gert Rosenthal, former Permanent Representative of Guatemala to the UN*

'This unique guide for negotiators syntheses the main insights a diplomat often only learns the hard way. It is a very much needed resource. Through this book, anyone interested in the work of the UN will be able to better understand the challenges of finding critical pathways, beyond culture and interests, to find workable solutions and common ground.'

—*Paula Caballero, Managing Director, Climate and Water, Rare; former Director of Economic, Social and Environmental Affairs, Ministry of Foreign Affairs, Colombia*

'A helpful 'How To' guide for both newcomers and old-timers in the ever-more-important arena of multilateral negotiations. As the world grapples with global problems ranging from climate change to global health to international trade and development, the UN will be an essential forum to reaching necessary global agreements, and this slim volume provides both an operational road-map for the practitioner and a valuable window into the process for all interested observers.'

—*Jonathan Pershing, former US Special Envoy for Climate Change*

Negotiating at the United Nations

This book offers a comprehensive practitioner's guide to negotiating at the United Nations (UN).

Although much of the content can be applied broadly, the guide focuses especially on navigating multilateral negotiations at the UN. The book is a tool to help new UN negotiators, explaining basic negotiation concepts and offering insight into the complexities of the UN system. It can also serve as a playbook for cooperation for negotiators at any level, exploring the dynamics of relationships and alliances, the art of chairing a negotiation, and the importance of balancing the power asymmetries present in any multilateral discussion. In addition, the book proposes improvements to the UN negotiation process, looks at the impact of information technologies on negotiation dynamics, and shares stories from women UN delegates to illustrate what it means to be a female negotiator at the UN. This book is an exploration of the power of the individual in any negotiation, and of the responsibility all negotiators have in wielding that power to speak for a better world.

This book will be of much interest to students of diplomacy, global governance, foreign policy, and International Relations, as well as practitioners and policymakers.

Rebecca E. Webber Gaudiosi represented the United States at the UN from 2006–14, leading on U.S. engagement with over 25 organizations focused on environment and sustainable development. She has also worked with several UN specialized agencies and on bilateral environment issues. Her most recent assignment was at the U.S. Embassy in Cairo.

Jimena Leiva-Roesch was at the Permanent Mission of Guatemala to the UN in New York, from 2009–15, where she last served as Counsellor. She was the lead negotiator for Guatemala in the Sustainable Development Goals (SDGs) and UN climate change negotiations. She is currently a Research Fellow with the International Peace Institute.

Ye-Min Wu has worked with the Ministry of Foreign Affairs, Singapore for over a decade. While at the Permanent Mission of Singapore to the UN in New York, she chaired UN negotiations as well as represented the Group of 77 and China in UN negotiations on sustainable development issues. The views expressed herein are the views of the author and do not necessarily represent the views of the Government of Singapore.

Negotiating at the United Nations

A Practitioner's Guide

Rebecca E. Webber Gaudiosi,
Jimena Leiva-Roesch
and Ye-Min Wu

LONDON AND NEW YORK

First published 2019 by Routledge

2 Park Square, Milton Park, Abingdon, Oxfordshire OX14 4RN
52 Vanderbilt Avenue, New York, NY 10017

Routledge is an imprint of the Taylor & Francis Group, an informa business

First issued in paperback 2019

British Library Cataloguing in Publication Data
A catalogue record for this book is available from the British Library

Library of Congress Cataloging-in-Publication Data
Names: Webber Gaudiosi, Rebecca E., author. | Leiva Roesch, Jimena, author. | Wu, Ye-Min, author.
Title: Negotiating at the United Nations : a practitioner's guide / Rebecca E. Webber Gaudiosi, Jimena Leiva-Roesch and Ye-Min Wu.
Description: Abingdon, Oxon ; New York, NY : Routledge, 2019. | Includes bibliographical references and index. |
Identifiers: LCCN 2018047524 (print) | LCCN 2018059949 (ebook) | ISBN 9780429956720 (Web PDF) | ISBN 9780429956713 (ePub) | ISBN 9780429956706 (Mobi) | ISBN 9781138590410 (hardback) | ISBN 9780429491047 (e-book)
Subjects: LCSH: United Nations--Decision making. | International cooperation--Decision making. | Negotiation.
Classification: LCC JZ4984.5 (ebook) | LCC JZ4984.5 .W44 2019 (print) | DDC 341.23--dc23
LC record available at https://lccn.loc.gov/2018047524

ISBN: 978-1-138-59041-0 (hbk)
ISBN: 978-0-367-43477-9 (pbk)

Typeset in Sabon
by Taylor & Francis Books

To our children – the future negotiators for a better world – and our supportive husbands, without whom we could not have written this book.

Soli Deo Gloria

Contents

Illustrations

Figures

Boxes

Foreword

This is a very useful book on United Nations (UN) negotiations. Diplomats, young and old, being assigned to work in the UN system for the first time will find this a helpful guide. I thank Wu Ye-Min, Rebecca E. Webber Gaudiosi and Jimena Leiva-Roesch, the co-authors of this brilliant book for giving me the privilege of contributing the foreword to this book.

The three authors are three young women, from Singapore, the United States and Guatemala, respectively, who have served with distinction at the UN. It is wonderful that an Asian, an American, and a Latin-American can transcend so many boundaries and work so well together. The world needs more people like Ye-Min, Rebecca and Jimena.

While the UN is an imperfect organization, it has helped to create a safer and better world that is governed by laws, rules and principles. The UN Charter's objectives include the development of international law, the protection of human rights, the prevention of war, and the promotion of economic and social progress. With the UN, states, big and small, are held accountable for their actions towards other countries as well as towards their own citizens. All countries, big or small, wish to live in a peaceful and stable world. We also all aspire to live in a world governed by law rather than by force.

Negotiation is an essential part of a diplomat's life. This is especially true when a diplomat is posted to a multilateral institution like the UN or WTO. Having done hundreds of negotiations, both bilateral and multilateral, in my career, I have come to the conclusion that negotiation is both an art and a science. What makes a good negotiator? In my opinion, a good negotiator must have warmth, competence, integrity and fair-mindedness. A negotiator with all four qualities will be a good negotiator. In fact, she would often be sought after by her peers to assume the role of facilitator, convener or chairwoman.

This book is an excellent guide for negotiators in the UN system. The book has excellent content and is written in a clear, reader-friendly and entertaining style. For these reasons, I am confident that it will be a great success.

Tommy Koh
President, UN Conference on the Law of the Sea, 1981–1982
Chairman, Main Committee and Preparatory Committee,
UN Conference on Environment and Development, 1990–1992
Singapore's Chief Negotiator,
The US-Singapore Free Trade Agreement, 2001–2003

Foreword

"Efficiency" is admittedly not the first word that comes to mind when we think of the discussions that take place in the halls of the United Nations (UN). But is efficiency the purpose of UN discussions? While operational efficiency is an attribute that the UN has improved upon slowly over the past 70 years and should continue to improve, it is not core to achieving the purpose of the institution. The UN promotes matters that are above efficiency: peace, human rights and sustainable development in all its forms. Those colossal goals are pursued on the basis of fundamental fairness among all Member States, and fairness can only evolve when all nations have an equal chance to express their interests and needs – often diametrically opposed – and then move toward a middle ground that allows everyone to gain something, and no one to take everything. That process cannot be pursued with simple "efficiency." To be effective, that process has to be understood as an art as well as a science. It is tedious, complex and challenging, but it is immensely rewarding and it is what is at the heart of all negotiations under the UN.

As Executive Secretary of the UN's Framework Convention on Climate Change (UNFCCC) from 2010 to 2016, including the delivery of the Paris Agreement, I am keenly aware of the difficulties of crafting a global agreement. However, outcomes such as the 2030 Agenda and the Paris Agreement represent not only amazing achievements in defiance of all odds, but also attest to the fact that the UN can be effective. It can be the platform upon which countries build fair and ambitious political frameworks that chart a concrete and meaningful path forward for humanity.

The authors of this book have written an essential guide for anyone interested in understanding the complex nature of multilateral negotiations. The book reveals key insights and lessons that negotiators typically come to understand only after many years of practical experience. This book speeds up the learning process for those interested in making the UN a more effective platform to tackle global challenges. It offers a holistic sense of what it means to be a UN negotiator – from the global South or the global North – as well as presenting the nuanced challenges that come with the varying country or group positions. It also brings a unique perspective not often discussed in the halls of the UN: what does it mean to be a female negotiator in yet another male dominated workplace? As one of the few women from the global South who has reached a top-level leadership position at the UN, I firmly believe that it is important not only to be more open about gender differences but also to explore how female leadership can enhance negotiations.

This book covers a breath of topics that are explicitly practical, including such essentials as how to build alliances and how to successfully chair a meeting. The authors describe the different power dynamics at play between countries North and South, big and small. Such discussions cannot be found in any college textbook or academic context. This book is unique in its class because it is written by seasoned UN negotiators. Drawing from their wealth of experience, the authors describe how negotiators can be successful – they present what it takes to craft complicated agreements such as the 2030 Agenda for Sustainable Development and the Paris Agreement. It is an invaluable guide for complex negotiations that will undoubtedly arise in the future.

In the current geopolitical context, it is even more important that negotiators learn as quickly as possible how to communicate and work across cultures and political differences in order to find agreement. Having reached planetary boundaries on all levels, we have no other recourse but to find multilateral solutions to our growing challenges, and the strength of our multilateral institutions depends ultimately on how effectively we use them.

Christiana Figueres
Former Executive Secretary of the
UN Framework Convention on Climate Change

The story behind this book

It had been a morning of tough negotiations at the Governing Council of the United Nations (UN) Environment Programme in Nairobi, Kenya. When we met each other at break time, we laughed over coffee about the idea of putting our negotiation war stories in a book someday.

We day-dreamed of writing a book that would combine the perspectives of three female negotiators representing three very different countries: Guatemala, Singapore, and the United States. Together, we had learned first-hand, through some tears and much laughter, that negotiating among 193 UN Member States is a frustrating, exhausting, and wonderful experience that – if done right - can yield transformative results for the world.

Former UN Secretary-General Dag Hammarskjöld understood the tension that exists between national interests and service to the world. Like many other diplomats, he often struggled with these contrasting ideals. Nevertheless, he believed the UN was the place where, "it is possible to serve the world by serving our nation, and to serve our nation by serving the world."[1] He believed any negotiator could learn how to *speak for the world* by balancing national interests and global responsibility.

Speaking for the world is not an easy undertaking, especially in the context of competing national and global priorities, but we strongly believe the ability to do so is within reach for those who aspire to it. We also believe national and global priorities do not have to be in competition; our personal experience has taught us that when we work with others to reconcile what may at first appear to be conflicting interests, we can achieve groundbreaking results. The idea for this book is therefore threefold:

First, that new negotiators to the UN would not have to learn the lessons we did the hard way, starting from zero. With a guidebook that could help jump-start their UN negotiation journey, they could ease more quickly into their negotiator role, avoid the standard mistakes, and have the power to bring more positive global change through diplomacy. We wanted to offer negotiators a tool to reduce the learning curve.

Second, that negotiators will be able to see how others before them had crossed geographical, cultural, and ideological divides to build outcomes – together – that could benefit the greater good. By drawing on others' stories and experiences, negotiators facing their own battles would be able to draw inspiration and strength to find common ground. We wanted to offer a playbook for cooperation.

Third, that everyone will recognize their own power and responsibility as a negotiator and use it to speak for a better world. Negotiations – regardless of the flag you represent – are a deeply personal experience: you carry your own stories, values, and personality with you into the process. Each individual influences the negotiation and the outcome more than you might ever imagine. Negotiations are not limited to the UN domain, they take place regularly in everyday life. We can speak to tear others down, or we can speak to build them up. We hope this book helps readers to do the latter.

This book is written by three negotiators; it is therefore not a book on theory, but on practice. It is a handbook for negotiators and anyone interested in understanding how complex multilateral agreements are made. Although much of the content can apply more broadly, it is especially a guide to navigating the turbulent waters of multilateral negotiations at the UN. We hope you will find it multilayered: informative for the young diplomat just starting her career, while a helpful companion to the experienced negotiator who will see a reflection of her own experience (and a reminder of the associated lessons) in its pages.

Like many UN negotiation drafts, we see this book as a "live" document and would welcome constructive feedback on how we can improve it! You can contact us at: 3femalenegotiators@gmail.com.

Note

1 Kai Falkman, *To Speak for the World: Speeches and Statements by Dag Hammarskjöld, Secretary-General of the United Nations 1953–1961* (Stockholm: Atlantis, 2005), 142.

Acknowledgments

This book would not have been possible without our friendship. We found each other at the UN, where we worked together to make a difference, for our countries, and hopefully, the world. As a start, we would like to thank Andrew Humphrys and his team at Routledge for taking a chance on us! We would like to acknowledge with gratitude the frameworks used by CMPartners, LLC and Chris Argyris that we discuss in this book. We sincerely appreciate the input from a long list of contributors and informal editors, including: Stephanie Aktipis, Josefina Bunge, Juanita Castano, Chan Yu-Ping, Lynne Gadkowski, Kartika Handaruningrum, Rueanna Haynes, Ryan Lee Hom, Benito Jimenez-Sauma, Agnieszka Karpińska, Farrukh Khan, Denise McQuade, Ntesang Molemele, Karthik Nachiappan, Ambassador Namira Negm, Natalia Novoa, Ambassador Nadia M. Osman, Urawadee Sriphiromya, Jakob Ström, Claire Thuaudet, Tok Xinying, Dewi Savitri Wahab, Schuyler Weiner, and Nicholette Williams. We especially offer thanks to Elizabeth Cousens for her insightful input, Christiana Figueres for her contribution, Ambassador Tommy Koh for his advice and contributions, and Elizabeth McClintock for her negotiation and editorial insights. A big thank you goes to Mathieu de Muizon for the lovely vignettes scattered throughout!

JLR: To my daughter Maxima, whom I birthed and nursed through this process and to manman for holding my hand in sunny days and carrying me in rainy days. With thanks to my parents, from whom I learned the first lessons on negotiation! With gratitude to Ambassador Rosenthal and peers at the Mission of Guatemala for your trust and lessons in speaking for Guatemala and for a better world.

WYM: To Mom, Dad, Tim, Eli, Emi and Ganma, my deepest appreciation for your unfailing love, support and patience over the years! To friends and family, sincere thanks for enriching and supporting me through my journeys. My gratitude goes to Lena, NCC and Crossroad sisters for keeping this project in prayer. And thank you MFA bosses and colleagues, I have learnt so much from you all. Most importantly, to God be the glory. *Do nothing out of selfish ambition or vain conceit. Rather, in humility value others above yourselves, not looking to your own interests but each of you to the interests of the others. Philippians 2: 3–4 (NIV)*

REWG: Deepest thanks to my family (mom, dad, and Adam), for their generous and unflagging support over many long years, leading up to where I am today. Special thanks to my brilliant husband, whose insights and creative ideas enliven every day and every project. Many thanks to all of my colleagues and counterparts over the years, from whom I have learned so very much. Special appreciation goes to the AAAS, George (who, during my third week in my first job, sent me to NY), Doug and Jason (who pushed me in), Bill and Andrew (who helped empower me), Lynne and Stephanie (my support group), and the U.S. Delegation to Rio+20. The Rio+20 process stole my mid-thirties, but taught me many lessons and gave me so many, many friends – thanks to all of you, I can't wait to work together again!

Introduction

When the United Nations (UN) is united, it sends a strong signal to the world and sets the direction for action. This is because the UN is the sum of its Member States' values and positions. It is as strong or as weak as its membership allows it to be. As such, when UN Member States operate together towards a common purpose, the UN becomes greater than the sum of its parts, with the potential to achieve the loftiest aspirations for sustainable living in a peaceful world. Communities worldwide recognize the UN as a (if not, the most!) representative global body, giving it a unique legitimacy. Negotiators sent to the UN to discuss global challenges understand the value of the organization and their role there. One therefore expects UN negotiators to be engaged daily in meaningful negotiations, producing action-oriented outcomes, and spending breaks singing kumbaya. Instead, UN negotiators often find themselves in a time loop of unnecessary drama and needless debate.

A seasoned negotiator can predict how the UN debate will go and what the compromise outcome will look like even before delegations have made their statements. The repeated discussions, dynamics, and accompanying theatrics between the various UN parties follow a well-known script, read time and time again by different actors. For example, the heated debates at the preparatory meetings for the 2012 UN Conference on Sustainable Development on developed versus developing country responsibilities for environmental protection are eerily similar to those in advance of the 1972 UN Conference on the Human Environment. However, because of the importance of these issues, UN delegates often insist on tiring themselves out rehashing old arguments before they are willing to accept the often-obvious compromise.

There are periods during which negotiators at the UN have managed to break free from the repetitive dynamics to reach important global agreements, such as the Sustainable Development Goals and the Paris Agreement on climate change. Both outcomes are the fruit of creative, multi-year negotiation processes in which the traditional script was not followed. And both agreements now chart a way forward for generations to come – changing the way business is being conducted, improving sustainable consumption and production patterns, and offering a common language on sustainable development.

The perception of the UN has also changed over its 70-year lifespan. To the outside observer, the UN may no longer be viewed as an esteemed council of wise men, but rather as an overly expensive enterprise of dubious necessity, at best, or simply a failure, at worst. For many, the UN is almost like health insurance: some gripe over their health insurance premiums while others wonder if they need insurance at all, until an unexpectedly bad medical report comes in, and the presence of a safety net suddenly becomes important to the afflicted patient. Priorities have changed, and it seems obvious that health insurance is essential; the patient wonders why there are not more people focused on this vital subject. The UN suffers a similar plight.

The immediate value of the UN is most apparent to people in severe distress. For the two billion people living in countries under stress or in conflict zones, the UN remains a symbol of hope that justice will be served and that they will someday enjoy the fruits of peace taken for granted in other parts of the world. Just one of these is Sopheak, aged eight, whom we have learned about from UN staff; she dreams of attending school but is trapped working for the human trafficker to whom her impoverished and desperate parents sold her. The UN is a first responder and standard setter. That said, protracted international conflicts are leaving some youth disillusioned with the UN for not acting swiftly enough "to save succeeding generations from the scourge of war,"[1] the main reason for the UN's formation.

The work of the UN goes beyond feeding the hungry and sheltering the homeless – what is most featured in mainstream media and funding campaigns – and many of the UN's most important activities go unnoticed. The UN and its agencies prevent epidemics like Ebola and SARS from spreading. With more satellites being used for navigation, communications, and weather apps on our cell phones, the UN's Committee on the Peaceful Uses of Outer Space is busy addressing the long-term sustainability of outer space activities. Almost 90 percent of global fish stocks are overfished or fully fished; the UN's Food and Agriculture Organization develops important conservation agreements to ensure that our children will have seafood to eat. The UN's International Atomic Energy Agency tackles the Zika virus by sterilizing male insects, uses irradiation to help farmers to improve plant varieties, and increases patient access to the latest advances in radiotherapy for cancer care. In all these important areas, the UN partners with other stakeholders, such as foundations, civil society organizations, governments, and the private sector, as it can neither operate in a silo nor do it alone.

The UN and its myriad meetings also provide a crucial platform for global dialogue and cooperation. The UN General Assembly gives each country, independent of size and power, a voice. The UN has thus served, and continues to serve, as a key channel for de-escalating conflict relating to issues of sovereignty, politics, and competitive bilateral dynamics. Moreover, the UN provides the space and opportunity for opposing parties to build positive relations. This critical role of maintaining peace is often taken for granted. Without the hard work of UN negotiators and mediators in preventive diplomacy, our world could be mired in even more conflict than what we presently see.

It is because of our strong belief in and experience with the UN that we offer our collective thoughts on participating in and improving the UN negotiation process in this book. For the UN to address global challenges effectively, UN negotiators must have the ability to negotiate productively and meaningfully to turn dialogue into outcomes. This book details how negotiators can overcome political, economic, and ideological divides to build solutions – solutions that address the issues of all sides and achieve positive outcomes. Drawing on a range of UN negotiations, from the General Assembly to the Security Council, we take you inside the world of the UN.

In the first part of the book, we review some basic negotiation concepts. Chapter 1, "Negotiating the Hard Stuff," illustrates how negotiators can establish their key interests and redlines. When negotiators come in with the mindset that they want what they want, and don't want what they don't like, they can erode the effectiveness and credibility of the UN and the world ends up on the losing end. Negotiators need to understand how to trade off less important issues at times in order to protect items that are at the top of their priority list. Sometimes, this can mean putting together a "package deal."

Unlike a tourist bargaining over a souvenir, UN negotiators negotiate issue A today and meet tomorrow to negotiate issue B, so a negotiator needs to guard her reputation and credibility like a prized possession. In an environment where information (including gossip) is power, a negotiator's reputation has the advantage (or disadvantage) of preceding her in a negotiation. Likewise, it is essential that a negotiator exude both warmth and competence, as research has shown those traits to be more likely to evoke help and cooperation from others.[2] This chapter details how negotiators can control their reputation and manage others' perceptions of them. It also explains what a real "win" looks like in a multilateral venue, achieved at times through understanding the psychology at work (such as the momentum of a negotiation), sending the right messages, and taking a well-timed pause.

Chapter 2, "Aren't Interests and Positions the Same Thing?," explains the common confusion over bargaining positions and interests in negotiations. The bargaining position is the narrative and strategy used to achieve one's interests. Simply put, when a child asks a parent to read another book before bedtime, it is not necessarily because the child is interested in that book or in reading in general. As the parent better understands the child, the parent knows the key interest in this situation is to defer bedtime.

To find a solution acceptable to another party, a negotiator must delve deeper than the stated position to find the underlying interests. Through case studies on UN negotiations, this chapter explains how one can distill others' words and actions to reveal these key interests. This requires empathy, patience, and the use of the "ladder of inference"[3] – effective inquiry, coupled with structured advocacy – to enable the negotiator to learn more about what her counterpart wants and needs, while offering the negotiator the opportunity to explain her own priorities. This is, essentially, the difference between talking to each other and talking at each other – highlighting the power of the negotiator as an individual. The chapter also explains how negotiators can be more self-aware to better mitigate the distractions and natural biases that can keep them from seeing possible solutions and potential allies in a negotiation.

The second part of the book helps the negotiator understand the peculiarities of the UN negotiation system and offers insight into successful navigation of its sometimes-rocky terrain. Chapter 3, "The Insider's Guide to the UN Negotiation System," details the structures in which a UN negotiation takes place and presents the complex process of drafting, tabling, and adopting UN resolutions. It demonstrates how negotiators can identify the timeline for decision-making, the key personalities involved in the negotiation, and the negotiation's history.

The chapter also provides examples of the unique language and concepts used in UN negotiations, such as "nothing is agreed until everything is agreed" and "placing a document under silence procedure." It delves into wordplay, including code words, showing how subtle differences in the word choice employed in a resolution can significantly impact the agreement – both its meaning and whether there is one at all. Additionally, this chapter describes tactics for optimal outcomes and some key methods for obscuring policy disagreements in a UN text. These include (i) using "agreed language," that is, phrases from resolutions previously adopted by the UN; (ii) "cancelling out" conflicting proposals by deleting all proposals on the issue so that all parties are equally unhappy; and (iii) using vague language that leaves everyone equally perplexed and partially satisfied.

At the UN, it does "take a village" to get the job done, and relationships are certainly one of the keys to success in multilateral negotiations. Chapter 4, "Don't Go it Alone: Building Relationships and Alliances," looks at how a negotiator can build good working relationships and optimally, alliances, to serve her interests. Regardless of how well developed a proposal may be, it can easily get blocked in a UN negotiation just because it is tabled by the "wrong" delegation. This can be due to a spillover effect from negotiators' inability to distinguish between the flag, the individual, and the issue, or because other negotiators do not know (or like, or respect) the proponent. (Hence, the importance of the negotiator as an individual!)

This chapter looks at the essential categories of relationships a negotiator will confront (and should court): friendlies (delegations with similar views); opposites (delegations with differing views); key personalities (which include power players, problem solvers, and spoilers); and quiets and neutrals (often, the majority). This chapter delves into how and why alliances are built at the UN. It also offers tips that negotiators can add to their networking toolkit to build appropriate rapport with others in a negotiation. The chapter closes with a discussion of UN negotiating groups – a particular sort of alliance – including the benefits and challenges of membership in large groups and their utility in and impact on negotiations.

Chapter 5, "Welcome to Negotiations Theatre: an Off-Broadway Production," presents the choreography of the official and unofficial portions of a multilateral negotiation. It is an open secret that most UN agreements are devised outside of formal UN meetings. This chapter explains the importance of "behind-the-scenes" negotiations, detailing how unofficial processes can be used to move a negotiation forward, including to brainstorm options and piece together a final deal, and illustrates how to effectively conduct them. It also describes the relationship a negotiator has with her capital, yet another counterpart in a UN negotiation.

The chapter describes the essential elements of a formal UN meeting – both the formal and informal components. It offers insight into the instrumental pageantry – taking place both behind the scenes and at the table – known as "negotiation theater." Posturing, acting, and recreating (or acting out) the compromise can be essential to the legitimacy of a UN outcome; they can also help communicate a delegation's message, counteract a spoiler, or convince an intractable delegate. This chapter underlines the importance of keeping one's emotions in check and depicts how emotional displays, and the use of overly theatrical tactics, can impact a negotiator's all-important reputation and credibility. It offers advice on using instructions from capital in a dynamic that can be similar to a negotiation. It also explains how every difficult conversation in a negotiation is about one or more of these three categories – facts, face, and feelings.[4]

Chapter 6, "I Call this Meeting to Order: Chairing UN Negotiations," discusses the key role that the Chairperson (Chair for short) plays in a negotiation. The chapter explains the tools a Chair can use to successfully steer the negotiation, including drafting, timing, and process management. It illustrates the importance of a Chair's credibility and integrity to a multilateral process and describes how a Chair can protect these essential assets with the appropriate conduct.

This chapter discusses how a Chair can leverage all the available resources to facilitate an outcome appropriate to the collective level of ambition. At certain times in a negotiation, she might need to be more commanding, and at others, she may need to step back. For example, offering too many suggestions to break deadlocks can lead negotiating parties to rely too much on the Chair; on the other hand, negotiators may "riot" when they view the Chair as controlling, rather than mediating, the dialogue. Such missteps can erode confidence in the eventual outcome. As chairing a UN negotiation is very much a personal role, the negotiator as an individual again comes into play; equal to a delegate's, but different, a Chair has power and responsibility. This chapter describes several types of Chairs, neutral, biased, and Chair-as-host, as well as some of the potential pitfalls that Chairs should avoid when taking on this esteemed (and sometimes, thankless) role.

Chapter 7, "Mitigating Asymmetric Power: the 800-pound Gorilla and the Fearless Ant," discusses the presence of asymmetric power in UN negotiations, as well as the challenges and opportunities that come with being a larger ("gorilla") or smaller ("ant") country. It discusses how delegates from smaller states can effectively overcome challenges they may face at the UN, – including limited influence, making themselves heard, and relative capacity – to become key multilateral actors. By leveraging their strengths – among them, a relative nimbleness – this chapter shows how "ant" delegates can champion their countries' interests at the UN, while having impacts larger than their "size" on negotiation processes and outcomes.

It also discusses how Member States – or individual delegates – can become a "gorilla," and why this can be not only detrimental to a successful outcome, but also a burden for the negotiator. Although a "gorilla" has relative advantages, how a delegate uses these can significantly impact a multilateral process. This chapter explains the need for a "gorilla" delegate to be aware of her potential impact on a negotiation and suggests ways to counteract the imbalance. This chapter demonstrates how "gorilla" and "ant" delegates can both overcome the perceptions associated with their size to minimize power disparities and achieve outcomes acceptable to all. It underlines again that the individual negotiator can matter, as much, if not more than the flag in a UN negotiation.

The last part of the book explores ideas and issues that we feel are "in progress," and on which we hope to see future discussions in the context of UN negotiations. In Chapter 8, "I am a Female Negotiator: So What?," we share stories by women UN delegates across the globe about their experiences negotiating at the UN. Through their voices, we illustrate what it means to be a female negotiator at the UN, particularly how being a woman can have an impact on the dynamics and outcomes of a negotiation.

Through their anecdotes and experiences, this chapter explores how women at the UN see themselves and, in their views, how others perceive them. Their stories convey that gender stereotypes continue to play a role in the multilateral sphere, and that the UN – despite some excellent work on women's issues – is not a refuge from sexism. Additionally, the concept of women and related issues remain political in the UN context. Some of the stories convey that women may approach negotiations differently (and in some cases, more effectively) than men. Some women shared that they experienced more self-doubt than their male colleagues appeared to, or that they had to work harder to earn respect. Others felt less strongly about their gender playing any role in their UN experience. In presenting some women-specific challenges and opportunities, the anecdotes also offer strategies that female negotiators have used at the UN to overcome obstacles in a male-dominated world.

Chapter 9, "Please Excuse Us as we Update our Process … and Software," addresses some of the problems we have identified with the current method of negotiating resolutions at the UN, especially during the General Assembly. This chapter focuses on ways to improve the process, namely: (i) reduce the number of resolutions tabled each year and bring more focus to each resolution; (ii) encourage a culture of innovation; and (iii) provide more training for negotiators, particularly through simulation exercises.

This chapter also discusses a number of ways in which digital technology has had an impact on multilateral negotiations. Real-time communications, social media, and online content have significantly altered the way UN business is conducted, with both positive and negative results. While digital diplomacy and online content can increase transparency with the public and garner greater buy-in for UN agreements beyond just the governments of Member States, social media tools have influenced confidentiality and timelines in negotiations at the UN and altered the dynamics. Communication apps have improved the connections between delegates, but can also serve to distract delegates from the face-to-face conversations that remain essential to multilateral negotiations as they are currently conducted. Likewise, real-time communications have improved a delegate's connection to capital; that said, they don't always serve to empower delegates on the ground. Technology offers great potential and significant change; a savvy delegate should pursue its best uses. This chapter encourages the UN negotiator to improve the "process," however, and whenever, possible.

The concluding chapter summarizes the key lessons from each chapter. It also focuses on the lessons of former UN Secretary-General Dag Hammarskjöld, who believed that every individual involved in international relations, particularly those working with the UN, should speak for the world, rather than from purely national interest. It is a privilege to have a voice at the negotiation table and an effective negotiator can have tremendous impact; the true negotiator is a leader. As the world confronts complex challenges, a new generation of leaders is needed to speak across cultures and national interests. This will enable the international community to address global challenges more effectively and produce the best outcomes for the people of the world.

We all negotiate. The negotiations may be with colleagues about timelines or with our families about dinnertime. We negotiate so often that we do not always realize when we are in a negotiation. This book explains how we can make our negotiations more effective and meaningful, whether at the UN or elsewhere. It is dedicated to anyone who dreams of negotiating for a better world, on any scale.

Notes

1 United Nations, *Charter of the United Nations*, 24 October 1945.
2 Craig Lambert, "The Psyche on Automatic," *Harvard Magazine*, November-December 2010 (2010), http://harvardmagazine.com/2010/11/the-psyche-on-automatic.
3 Originally created by Chris Argyris and simplified by CMPartners, LLC for practitioners' use in negotiating and communicating.
4 Douglas Stone, Bruce Patton, and Sheila Heen, *Difficult Conversations: How to Discuss What Matters Most* (New York: Penguin, 2011), Kindle edition.

Part One

Negotiator Tool-Kit

1 Negotiating the hard stuff

Disclaimer: The stakes at the UN are certainly more serious than those in a board game. Nevertheless, like simulation exercises used for negotiating training, envisioning a game can help the new negotiator understand some of the basic dynamics of a tough UN negotiation. Like experienced gamers who know where to find all the traps and extra resources to gain temporary invincibility in a game, an experienced negotiator knows how to navigate the negotiation terrain, avoid pitfalls, and attain resources to boost her chances of forging a good outcome.

In this chapter, we provide a tongue-in-cheek instruction manual for playing the "game" known as "The Difficult Negotiation." While we prefer interest-based negotiation over positional bargaining, this is a situation you may encounter at some point in your life and it is important for you to build awareness of the terrain. Take courage that others have gone down this road before and good luck!

The difficult negotiation: What trade-offs will you make? Will the parties emerge victorious?

Overview

The game is often played over several rounds. In each round, each player (negotiator) chooses a role and takes one or more actions. For example, a player can choose the role of "The Intransigent" and take the action of "Belabouring Arguments."

Through roles and actions, the player aims to secure her priorities, without crossing any of her red lines. Points are won by securing priorities. Points are lost when ceding priorities. If a player crosses her red line, she immediately loses the game. Special victory points are awarded when an action makes the world a better place.

At the end of the last round, each player votes on whether she would like, in future, to play this game again with each of the other players. If the majority votes no against a player, that player loses the game immediately. This usually happens when the player has lost trust and goodwill over the course of the game.

The main aim for each player is to make the best choices on roles and actions, while making and maintaining good working relationships. At the end of the game, every player counts up their points. If every player is above zero, every player wins. If any player is below zero, every player loses.[1]

Game components

The roles

- The Intransigent: Refuses to change her mind
- The Bridge-Builder: Tries to help two or more other parties secure their interests without crossing her own red lines
- The Derailer: Keeps the parties from moving forward
- The Know-It-All: Has something to say about everything
- The Meanie: Put on your scariest face and scare them into submission
- The Earnest Newbie: Appear clueless in the hope that others will treat you gently
- The Indifferent: Look up and nod your head between intervals of instagramming
- The Blusterer: Like a sharp-elbowed pedestrian on a crowded street or a bull in a china shop, go ahead and burn those relational bridges!
- Players are welcome to create new roles for themselves.

The actions

- Discuss
- Offer advice
- Offer clearly unwanted advice
- Confer among selected players
- Collaborate among selected players
- Make a proposal
- Accept an offer
- Pretend you are paying attention
- Stall
- Belabour arguments
- Renege on an agreement
- Throw a hissy fit
- Walk away
- Players are welcome to create new actions for themselves.

Playing the game

Choosing roles

When choosing roles, players should aim for roles that exude both warmth and competence. As Harvard Business School professor Amy Cuddy and other experts have found, people evaluate new people they meet based on their warmth and competence.[2] Those seen to be competent but cold may evoke envy and resentment by others. Those perceived as warm and competent are more likely to receive help and cooperation. Those who appear to be warm but less competent are often treated as non-competitors (hence the occasional advantage of the role of Earnest Newbie).

Establish priorities

At the start of the game, each player should establish priorities that represent her interests. Identify how important each priority is to you. For example, you can give each priority a number from 1–10, 1 for "a nice to have" and 10 for "I will implode without this."

In a negotiation, you are likely to have to make trade-offs. Trade-offs involve giving up an item to receive another in return. Knowing how valuable each item is to you – or how to achieve your interests in an alternative way – helps you to make calculated trade-offs.

Next, identify your red lines. These are items seriously detrimental to your interests. If you agree to it, or anything worse, you are better off walking away from the negotiation. For example, some people refuse to date nose-pickers. To them, dating a person who relishes nose-picking in public crosses a red line.

Each player may have different priorities and red lines. To plan your trade-offs, you need to understand the other parties' priorities and red lines. This involves using the "ladder of inference" – effective inquiry, coupled with structured advocacy – which will allow you to learn more about what your counterpart(s) want and need, while offering you an opportunity to explain your priorities (explained in Chapter 2).

Shared priorities and/or red lines are opportunities for building alliances (see Chapter 4). Different priorities and/or red lines are opportunities for making trades or creating solutions where both parties can benefit. There is a well-known story in negotiations about satisfying two people who wanted the same orange. The two parties wanted the orange – but one for the juice, the other for the peel. Evidently, having different interests does not always need to lead to a fight.

Some players come to the negotiating table with the mindset of wanting what they want, and not wanting what they don't like. This limits the opportunities for trades and creating solutions together. Say two players want the orange for the juice. The intractable player demands the whole orange and is unwilling to compromise. The other player who wants the juice can try to sell the peel to buy more oranges, concede the orange, or hold fast and see who blinks first. It is one thing to play who blinks first with an orange, it is another to do so at the UN when lives are at stake.

Making trades

The game often boils down to players trading off some of their less important priorities to secure the priorities at the top of their respective lists, while forging common solutions based on their interests.

In early rounds, a player may wish to focus on items where agreement can be easily reached, also known as "low hanging fruit." These can be items low on both parties' priority lists, or where the trade-off or common interest is quite clear for both sides, and one that players are keen to make. Such "low hanging fruit" can help players build trust and confidence in each other, essential elements during the more complex rounds. But beware of exhausting your resources to secure low level priorities – significant resources (e.g. goodwill, energy and time) are likely to be needed when negotiating high level priorities.

Another approach is to request priorities that seem comparatively inconsequential to the other party after the latter has made a large concession. Concessions usually involve giving up something of value. Having given up something expensive, this player is likely to make the second concession as well since the latter now seems much less valuable (and thus feels less painful) in comparison. This is likely why McDonald's upsize meals are attractive. Having paid say $5.45 for a Big Mac meal, the 50 cents cost of upsizing seems like a steal in comparison! For another UN negotiator's take on making trades, see "Strategic Planning: Negotiating and Conceding in Your Favor" by Ryan Lee Hom at the end of this chapter.

Package deals

Package deals can be used to encourage trade-offs, particularly if more incentives are needed for concessions to be made. As a basic example of this, Viv wants to borrow her colleague Joe's car tonight so she can meet friends for dinner. She offers to take his night shift at work tomorrow. It is a one-for-one trade. Joe ups the bargain, he wants Viv to take two night shifts. Viv has been eyeing Joe's new video game, she packages the deal by offering to take two of his night shifts at work for the use of his car and new video game. He agrees and it is a win for both parties!

At the climate talks in advance of the Paris Agreement, one of the most complicated issues was asking large developing economies to reduce their emissions of greenhouse gases because this was perceived as asking them to stop or slow their economic growth. As such, a package deal was proposed to satisfy the various interests of the negotiating parties. It included financial support for developing countries as well as the space for countries to declare voluntarily their contributions to decrease greenhouse gas emissions.

Players can therefore consider how priorities can be grouped to make the trade-offs acceptable to the parties. Do note the downsides. If too many items are packaged in a deal, a failure of one can be a failure of all. Going back to our Viv and Joe example, Viv now offers to take four of Joe's night shifts at work if he gives her the pair of movie tickets he won at the company's raffle last night. Joe's partner walks in and questions how he could have given away *their* movie tickets and drives off his car in a huff. Viv tries to renegotiate a new deal with Joe but Joe is now too upset to talk about any deals. A package deal that works is great; a package deal that does not work just makes the problem bigger.

Even seasoned players have thrown out the baby with the bathwater or tanked fruitful agreements because they overextended themselves in a package deal. After one Minister got preliminary agreement on his country's top priorities in a bilateral negotiation, he misread the response of his counterpart and tried to push for more. In the negotiation room, he said the deal did not fully address his country's concerns and called for his counterpart to make more concessions. It backfired and the bilateral meeting ended without any agreement.

Another example of a package deal going astray is the negotiations on anti-dumping at the Uruguay Round on multilateral trade. As Singapore's negotiator Margaret Liang recounts:

> However, the negotiations during the whole month of October did not make much progress given that the other major groups on agriculture, TRIPS (Trade-Related Aspects of Intellectual Property Rights), and services were still not in their final stages. The US and European Community were thus not ready to concede on anti-dumping.[3]

An item once entangled in a package deal cannot be easily untangled. A package deal can also slow down discussions on each item in the deal. As such, negotiators should try to ensure that a package deal does not affect any time-sensitive interests.

The psychological factor

In sports, we talk about psyching out the opponent. We train our brain so we do not inadvertently psych ourselves out. One Ambassador is known to listen to Rocky's fist-pumping theme to prepare his mindset before entering a negotiation room. This game is no different. Moderates, people who hold less extreme views, tend to negotiate with themselves (and their headquarters) before going to meet the other party. They weed out what they see as extreme and focus on middle ground proposals that seem feasible. People like working with moderates due to their practical and efficient nature. However, moderates may be at a psychological disadvantage when they trade with spoilers. This is because a spoiler moderates her bargaining position to a lesser extent than a moderate does. As a result, their opening proposals lack parity. This can skew the final outcome against the interests of moderates.

The same basic dynamic is evident in the simple debate between a dad and his six-year-old on the going rate of the tooth fairy. Moderate dad's instinct is $2 but he does his research (yes there is data on the internet on this) and offers the market rate of $3 a tooth. The six-year-old is saving up for a bike and demands $20 for her shaky tooth. Even if dad and child meet in the middle at $11.50, it is way off the market rate of $3 because the opening prices were $3 and $20, respectively.

Draconian mom arrives and laughs off dad's assumption that their child is not a tyrant. She knows that even if she offers the child one cent, the "middle ground" would still be around $10 if they both concede at the rate of $1 each round. She takes extreme action, declaring the tooth fairy out of business. The child, realising she has met her match, quickly drops her price to $10 then $5, before settling on the market rate of $3. Moderate dad realizes he needs to be more aware of how he thinks and how the other party thinks. Moreover, by partnering with draconian mom, he gets what he wants and comes out looking like the good guy! If there were 193 kids in the family, then we could begin to approximate the complexity a negotiator faces at the UN.

Momentum

Momentum is another psychological factor in negotiations. If most players appear to be in agreement, the one sitting on the fence is less inclined to object. A player tabling a proposal may thus wish to create the appearance of general agreement to dissuade potential naysayers (i.e. those who are unsure about the proposal but do not see it as a red line).

This can be done by having her allies on the subject speak up for the proposal at the negotiation table. A chorus of support creates a positive momentum that leaves potential naysayers thinking twice about the consequences of speaking against the proposal. However, once a party speaks against the proposal, the psychological barrier is broken and fence sitters now feel more emboldened to voice their views. Proponents should therefore engage potential naysayers on their concerns prior to the UN meeting to minimise their objections at the meeting.

This is why a rational proposal may fail at the UN. The majority agrees with the proposal, but is content sitting in silence. Those most vocal at the table are those against. Due to this chorus of voices (negative momentum), those who want to speak up for the proposal now have doubts. Meanwhile, those on the fence take into account who has spoken and assume that most countries are against the proposal.

The psychological factor affects the response of not just potential naysayers but also those clearly against the proposal. If the majority appears to be for a proposal at the UN, those clearly against may calibrate the manner in which they voice their objection. Examples of calibration are voicing concerns to the proponent in private instead of at the negotiation table (i.e. in public), and voting "abstain" instead of voting "no." Instead of calling for a vote, which they think they may lose, they may also let the proposal be adopted but read out a statement (e.g. explanation of vote in UN lingo) after its adoption to place on record their concerns.

The Negotiator's Pause[4]

During the game, it is important that players stop at intervals to review their roles and actions. This helps to ensure that they are on the right track to securing their top priorities. It is easy to get swept into the details of the negotiation and forget the big picture. This is why UN delegates joke that they are in their own world when they negotiate.

As recounted by Mr Sivakant Tiwari, one of Singapore's legal pioneers,

> One of the funniest stories of the Brussels Round is that so focused were we in our work (on negotiating TRIPS) that we did not even know that the Uruguay Round had collapsed. More than two hours after all the delegates had gone back to their hotels – in view of the failure of the Round – a Latin delegate walked into the Informal Working Group on TRIPS (IGWT) and asked what the IGWT was doing when the Brussels session had collapsed and everyone had gone back two hours earlier.[5]

Another example is when negotiators from the UN in New York arrived in Nairobi in 2011 for negotiations at the UN Environment Programme (UNEP). The New York-based and Nairobi-based negotiators had been negotiating the same subject of international environmental governance for the past months. All of the negotiations were supposed to feed into the UN Conference on Sustainable Development. However, the New York-based negotiators were surprised to find the Nairobi-based negotiators on a different track. It was like both set of negotiators were on different planets. There was no right or wrong, just the sheer realization that both sides needed to keep each other better informed at regular intervals since they were working on the same issue.

In contrast, in the lead up to the Paris Agreement on climate change (negotiated by experts at the UN Framework Convention on Climate Change, UNFCCC), delegates negotiating the Sustainable Development Goals in New York made a conscious effort to bridge what was being discussed in the two arenas due to overlaps in the subject matter.

The Negotiator's Pause is also very effective for use when the negotiator feels uncomfortable or upset in a negotiation, or is caught by surprise by her counterpart's statement or action. The co-authors found one of our negotiator friends in the hallway of a UNFCCC meeting taking such a pause. When asked why he was not in the meeting, he said he found himself getting angry when the speakers starting attacked him personally, even though he was just representing his country's interests. He had learnt it was unwise to negotiate when angry, and had therefore called his delegation teammate to take his seat for a while. The Negotiator's Pause can therefore be both a "scheduled" pause, as well as one that a negotiator learns to use in the heat of the moment to regain control of herself.

Clear messaging

Due to the complexity of this game, a solution may not always be clear to all players (assuming all players want a solution, which is not always the case). In such cases, players often weigh the odds before taking action. When calculating the odds, they try to interpret what is happening in the game, including the behavior and actions of the players. To avoid misinterpretation, it is important that each player's messages are clear. If you are vague, do so because you intend to be vague. Otherwise, other players may misread your intention and take an action that is not in your interest.

Such weighing-of-the-odds is also seen in international mediation. Parties in conflict calculate the risks of an action based on several factors, including the probability that the mediator and the international community as a whole will not respond to the conflict in the same manner. Mediators therefore need to reduce this probability as much as possible.

Former UN Secretary-General Kofi Annan's successful mediation of the political crisis in Kenya over the 2007 presidential election results shows the power of clear messaging. Annan understood that multiple mediators could lead to confusion. As he explained, "sometimes ministers come and speak to the parties and either one or the other side would take comfort from what they have said."[6] He therefore kept other mediators at bay and made it clear to the parties in conflict that there was only one mediating process. When UN Member States showed collective support for Annan's mediation, the parties in conflict realized that there would be no alternative option to Annan's proposals from the international community. This gave Annan important negotiating leverage vis-à-vis the parties in the mediation and allowed a viable solution that was universally respected. Annan's approach in the mediation demonstrated that the negotiator, and not just the flag, matters in international diplomacy. It also highlighted the power of UN unity.

Similarly, Special Envoys of the UN Secretary-General (SRSG) depend on the mandate given to them by the Secretary-General and the Security Council. If the Security Council stands united in a country situation and acts by consensus, that SRSG has more leverage in her work because of the unequivocal message sent by the Security Council. This is the case in many countries on which the Security Council has continued to have a united voice. For example, in Liberia, the UN mission there ended after 15 years of presence with considerable results. We have also witnessed the disastrous consequences of an unclear Security Council mandate, such as in Yemen and Syria.

Game end

At the end of the game, players think about whether they would like, in future, to play this game again with each of the other players. This is where the goodwill and trust built between players throughout the game, as well as "legacy" behaviors, play a crucial role.

In tense moments during the game, emotions can run high. Here, a player may exhibit "legacy" behaviors – so-called because her behavior is not easily forgotten, even if it is "out of character" for her. For example, she may make a mean comment in a fit of anger, or bang tables to get her way. Legacy behaviors affect her reputation and credibility. It also influences how other players respond to her in the future since players take action based on their interpretation of her behavior. Remember that individuals, and not just the flag, influence the negotiation! In an environment where information (including gossip) is power, a player's reputation has the advantage (or disadvantage) of preceding her in a negotiation. A player's reputation and credibility are thus her prized possessions.

Ten good actions may not wash away one legacy behavior. This is why the negotiator's pause and a keen awareness of one's behavior are important. Take a quick assessment of your state of mind at regular intervals during the game. Are you feeling tired? Are you feeling frustrated? Are you getting angry? If so, request a toilet break or ask your teammate to stand in for you for a few moments. A short break is worth your long-term reputation. Why "win" one game, in terms of priorities, only to have no one to play with again in future? That's equivalent to a loss: for that negotiator, her country, and for international cooperation.

Finally, check to see if the final outcome is implementable and if all players are committed to implementing the agreement. There is not much point in agreeing to something on paper if no one can, or is going to, do anything about it.

Strategic planning: negotiating and conceding in your favor[7]

By Ryan Lee Hom, Former Strategic Adviser on Development and Macroeconomic issues at the Permanent Mission of Papua New Guinea to the United Nations, and coordinator of the Group of 77 and China.

Is this good enough? Perhaps a question that we all ask ourselves on a daily basis, whether it's in your closet deciding what outfit to wear, or at the negotiating table figuring out if a deal will work for you. Like any scenario you may encounter, negotiations go two ways – you win some and you lose some. The key, of course, is to maximize gains while minimizing losses – we'll refer to them as concessions. To ensure the best possible outcome requires planning from the very first stages of a negotiation – using existing knowledge and a bit of foresight to turn the tables in your favor. However, you *will* have to concede at some point; the key is to know how to effectively plan so that you control what you concede, and when. And for the purposes of this article, we will assume that negotiations are conducted in a civil and cordial manner, devoid of any emotion and grounded purely in fact (almost never the case!), and that you are a 101 percent expert on every and anything pertaining to your negotiating topic.

But let's take a step back first. By its very nature, a concession is either a last resort option, or an extremely tactical move. Deciding whether or not to make a concession to begin with should be part of your plan from the very start, and should be one of the first things you consider. To determine this, you must establish what you think will be your "landing point," or where you think the final agreement will be. From here, you should establish your priorities. This is one of the most fundamental, and perhaps most important, parts of any sort of strategic planning. In order to win, you need to plan around a win. Being able to establish a realistic, yet ambitious, landing point will help you plan for the best possible outcome, as all future planning should stem from this. Further, this will allow you to adequately prepare for contingencies, be they in your favor or not.

To determine your priorities, you should seek to establish your "red lines" and "soft red lines." "Red lines" are your bottom lines, the things which you *must* get from a negotiation. These can also be used to demarcate the point at which you will walk away. "Soft red lines" are those priorities which are very important to you, and which you are willing to bargain for, but will not cause you to walk away from a negotiation. You should then categorically go through the rest of your objectives and prioritize them.

One particularly useful tactic is to establish some "false" or "loose" priorities. These are those issues which do not really matter to you, but which you hold onto for a tactical advantage, or as a bargaining chip. These will usually be sensible and carefully chosen, so as to ensure that your position makes sense to those on the other end of the negotiating table; further, these will also usually be an issue of significance to the other side, though not necessarily a red line of theirs. A hypothetical example of this could revolve around civil society and multi-stakeholder participation in meetings. One side, let's say side A, views multi-stakeholder participation as a fundamental position; while the other side, side B, is more or less indifferent to such participation, but has expressed some discomfort with such modalities in the past. Thus, side B decides to take the position against such participation, with the intention of conceding on this position later, but in exchange for something else which matters to them. In this case, side B is not really losing out, or making a "false concession" in order to leverage themselves into a better position.

Now that red lines and soft red lines have been established, and now that you've prioritized your objectives and set a few "false" priorities, it's time to trade off. However, in order to be able to effectively trade, you need to also know where your counterpart's priorities lie. Thus, doing the same thing you did for yourself, but for your counterpart is equally, if not more important, in order for you to be able to match up priorities and effectively negotiate packages. This is where knowing what and when to concede is crucial. Note that we're now talking about trading and not giving. Thus, any concession made should be to either build up a sort of "credit" which you can cash in on later, or be a direct trade for something else. This "credit" can be used as a show of flexibility used to persuade the other side that they have already gained something, and that they must show good faith and return the favor. In order to ensure the best possible outcome for yourself, you need not only to establish your priorities and objectives, but also to decide what sorts of alternative forms you are willing to accept your priorities in.

The key to negotiating is in ensuring that you play your cards in the right order. As a rule of thumb, try and close the easy issues first-either things that enjoy a good amount of consensus, or those things which can be quickly negotiated. This will allow you to zero in and focus on the bigger priorities, and force the other side to engage on these issues. It is also helpful to try and establish, before your counterpart does, how you would like to package certain issues (think back to getting where you want to end up, i.e. the landing point).

One of the most common pitfalls in negotiations is holding the mentality that you will get everything that you want. By definition, negotiations will entail a certain amount of give and take. Thus, in order to ensure maximal effectiveness, you want to ensure that you are asking for less than the other side is – or at least make it seem this way. One way to skew perceptions in your favor is to link issues. This will not only make it seem like you're asking for less, but that what you are asking for is perfectly sensible.

Another way to ensure that you get what you really want is to exchange many smaller priorities and "package" them together with a "red line" priority, or priorities. This is also where "false" priorities can come into play. You can use this "spare" bargaining chip to "sweeten a deal," which may need to be strengthened. However, you should seek to ensure that you are indeed giving a minimum amount. Thus, once you strike an initial deal, which is in line with your landing point, you should try and out-negotiate your counterpart, or "hold out" until the very last moment. You should also be careful not to keep too many of your own priorities on the table if you are planning to "hold out," as these "11th hour" deals often risk you losing out on whatever lesser priorities are left on the table.

Holding out is not necessarily a bad thing though. In fact, holding out at the right times is fundamental to any negotiation, and being able to let your counterpart "walk-in" your position. This means, having you slowly retreat from one "false red line" to the next, until you – though ideally you never will have to come this far – reach your actual red line. By doing this, you will be able to gauge your counterpart's willingness to be flexible and you can use this tactic to test the waters out.

The opposite of holding out, an alternative strategy which can be used to your advantage, is to concede early. By doing so, you will be perceived as being more flexible and reasonable, and might be able to spur your counterparts to start opening up and giving in on some of the objectives you are vying for. However, the key is not to give up too much, if you are the first to concede. This tactic will also depend on the dynamics of the negotiations, and more importantly the personal dynamics of the negotiators.

One thing that you should always be ready for, though cannot always plan for, is contingency scenarios. If you've done a good job of mapping out how a negotiation should go, according to both your and your counterpart's priorities, then you should be ready for almost, but not quite every, scenario. Thus, as another rule of thumb, it is always good to keep a few things, perhaps a false priority.

By the time you reach the end of a negotiation, you should have arrived close to, or exactly at, your landing point. If not, now would be a good time to look back, and see where you did not plan to be ambitious enough, or – what tends to be the case – where you were overly ambitious. Remember, that while being ambitious in a negotiation is important, being overly so might very well cause you to have to concede more than you would like. Thus, your ability to effectively and accurately plan will ultimately determine how good the outcome is for you. Being able to pick an accurate landing point is like any other acquired skill, which you will develop more over time as you get more exposure to negotiating, and as you learn more about both the topic and your own personal ability to negotiate. Aside from that, you just need a little good luck in not having to negotiate against an exceptionally emotional and short-fused counterpart!

Notes

1 If any one player comes away from a multilateral negotiation feeling like they lost – or having lost the respect and goodwill of others – this can easily affect the dynamic of future negotiations (for the individual and her delegation). As such, one player's "loss" has detrimental effects for the other players in future negotiations.

2 Craig Lambert, "The Psyche on Automatic," *Harvard Magazine*, November-December 2010 (2010), http://harvardmagazine.com/2010/11/the-psyche-on-automatic.

3 Margaret Liang, "Anti-Dumping Negotiations in the Uruguay Round," in *Economic Diplomacy*, ed. Margaret Liang and C.L. Lim (Singapore: World Scientific Publishing Co Pte Ltd, 2011), 71.
4 Adapted by CMPartners, LLC. Used with permission, 2018.
5 Sivakant Tiwari, "Intellectual Property Rights in the Uruguay Round," in *Economic Diplomacy*, ed. Margaret Liang and C.L. Lim (Singapore: World Scientific Publishing Co Pte Ltd, 2011), 85.
6 Martin Griffiths, "The Prisoner of Peace: An interview with Kofi A. Annan," *Centre for Humanitarian Dialogue* (2008), 5.
7 With Permission from Ryan Lee Hom.

2 Aren't interests and positions the same thing?

The four-year-old eyes the toy truck in his little sister's hands. He knows grabbing it from her hands will incur wrath from his parents. Instead, he picks up a plain building block, waves it in front of her, and pretends to fly it like a superfast spaceship. It catches her eye; she now wants this previously unattractive block. He hands it to her in a gesture of "brotherly love." Focused now on this "spaceship," she drops the toy truck and he runs off with it before she catches on to what is happening. Bingo! Brother has secured his interest without even revealing what it is.

Understanding your counterpart's interests is important for securing your own interests, whether you are four or ninety-four. It is also an element crucial to finding solutions acceptable to both (or more) parties in a negotiation. This chapter explains how negotiators can distill others' words and actions to decipher their counterparts' core interests and priorities. It discusses the difference between talking to each other and talking at each other, as the latter does little to persuade. The chapter also explains how to better manage the distractions and natural biases that can keep us from seeing potential solutions and potential allies in a negotiation.

Different sets of interests vs. bargaining positions[1]

Familiarity with your counterparts' interests, especially which set of interests tends to dominate in which situations, can help you see through their bargaining positions – the narrative and strategy they use to achieve their interests. Getting past this bargaining position is key to finding solutions that meet some of your counterpart's priorities.

To understand a person's interests, one must first get their perspective, as situations are rarely as simple as just wanting a toy truck, as in the example above. Take UN negotiator Janil from Country A, whose overall aim may be to promote and defend Country A's interests in a UN negotiation in support of a total ban on antipersonnel landmines in the Mine Ban Treaty. In achieving this overall goal, he has various sets of interests to balance, beyond the stated priorities of Country A, and these determine the actions he takes: Janil has flag or country interests – instructions from the foreign ministry of Country A, which has hopefully taken into account the views of other home agencies interested in the negotiation (ministries of finance, commerce, environment, health, etc.). Janil has delegation interests – he is supposed to take his cue from his Ambassador, who heads the delegation representing Country A in this negotiation. Janil also has personal interests – he generally prefers to avoid conflict (including at home and among his friends) and has views based on his moral principles on the use of landmines, which is the issue currently under negotiation. Ultimately, all these interests together influence what Janil says and does in a negotiation, including when and how hard he pushes for an issue.

In negotiations in which we have been involved, we have personally experienced, as well as seen other delegates grapple with, various sets of interests. At certain moments, consciously or unconsciously, one set of interests can come to dominate the others. We have listed some examples here based on our own experience.

Different sets of interests: case of strong personal interest

The negotiation outcome seemed fairly straightforward: the key issue had been battled-out the year before, countries had indicated no changes in their positions since, and the current draft resolution simply reiterated last year's outcome. It was therefore a big surprise when one delegate came in at the tail end of the brief negotiation process to say he wanted to change the characterization of last year's outcome (read: bargaining position). In side conversations, it emerged that a colleague from his delegation was equally surprised about this new position. Long story short, a lot of unnecessary time, sweat, and tears were shed in additional negotiation sessions to meet this delegate's demands, only for the outcome to return to its pre-drama state. After everything, the resolution reiterated the previous year's outcome, as expected. The "aha!" moment came years later when another friend remarked that this delegate had a penchant for last minute drama as he wanted to show he could influence the process (read: interest) and would often "blow up" negotiations in their final stages without good reason. Knowing in advance his strong personal interest over his delegation and country's interests would have better prepared us for the "blow up" in our negotiation.

Different sets of interests: case of strong country interest

The positions this female negotiator voiced in most negotiations were often rather extreme (read: bargaining position), resulting in long negotiation sessions within the group to find the "middle ground." After we became friends, she shared with us that her instructions from her foreign ministry, which she had to follow or she would lose her job, were very rigid, and she was very stressed out from constantly being in "fighting" mode (read: interests). With this knowledge in mind, we began to help her through one-on-one discussions to find solutions that her headquarters could accept. This reduced the lengthy and contentious debates within the group, earning goodwill from her, the chair, and other group members.

The person vs. the flag

Without an understanding of your counterpart's sets of interests, it is easy to confuse her bargaining positions with who she is and what she stands for. As a result, some negotiators take their counterpart's actions and statements personally, when the latter may have in fact been fronting an issue she herself did not believe in. In negotiations, it is worth heeding the advice of The Godfather, "It's not personal, Sonny. It's strictly business."[2]

The power of the individual

In the examples we have included throughout the book, you might begin to notice a common theme. The individual negotiator matters as much – or sometimes more than – the flag in a negotiation. How each delegate conducts herself in the negotiation, how she approaches a problem and interacts with colleagues, often dictates the outcome even more than country positions do. Negotiators defending conflicting positions but who collaborate well will likely reach a better negotiated outcome than negotiators who do not work well together.

Different sets of interests: case of strong delegation interest

The negotiators in the formal negotiation room seemed to be repeating their previously-stated positions (read: bargaining position) on this one outstanding issue in the document without coming any closer to agreement. The chair therefore called for a five minute break and asked to see the lead negotiators outside. Due to the strong rapport between these key players, one of the lead negotiators explained that he had instructions from his head of delegation to take a strong stand on this issue and not to budge from his initial position, even though a compromise proposed earlier by the chair was acceptable to his headquarters. This led another negotiator to explain that if others did not accept the chair's compromise first, she could not do so, even though it was acceptable to her delegation as well. This was because she would be seen by her delegation as "caving" (read: interest). This small group thus agreed among themselves that they would each display unhappiness over the chair's proposed compromise in the formal negotiation room before "grudgingly" accepting it as the outcome (see Chapter 5 for more on theatrics). This tactic successfully sealed the final deal in the negotiation. Thus, what a country conveys in public (its position) may not be its real interest.

"Ladder of inference"

Now that we know the difference between interests and bargaining positions, how can we learn enough information from the other party to distinguish between the two? Research published in the *Journal of Personality and Social Psychology*[3] indicates that "increasing interpersonal accuracy seems to require gaining new information rather than utilising existing knowledge about another person."[4] Further, the researchers concluded that "if you want to know what another person is thinking, it may be best to put them in a situation where they can answer honestly and then ask them directly."[5] It is therefore not sufficient to mentally "step into another's shoes" to understand another's perspective; it is essential to interact.[6] One of the most effective ways to do so is through the "ladder of inference" model originally created by Chris Argyris and simplified by CMPartners for practitioners' use in negotiating and communicating (see Figure 2.1).[7]

This approach focuses on the use of advocacy and inquiry when two or more people are communicating, while helping each party understand the realities the other is working with. Take Gerry and his friend Dan, who are arguing over who is the best tennis player of all time. Gerry's favorite is Roger Federer and Dan's is Andre Agassi. They have been talking up their favorite players for over an hour, but neither is convinced of the other's candidate (read: talking at each other). Riley is fed up with the ruckus and tells them to employ the "ladder of inference" (read: talking to each other). Dan begins by taking Gerry down Gerry's ladder, asking him why he thinks Federer is the best (read: inquiry mode). Gerry argues that Federer has the better career statistics (read: belief/

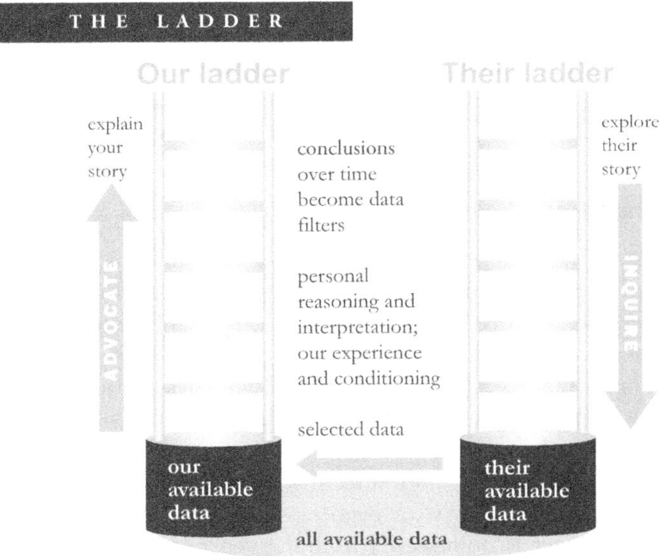

Figure 2.1 "Ladder of Inference"

interpretation). To Gerry, the number of important matches won defines a tennis player's achievements (read: assumption) and he pulls up both player's career statistics on the internet to show Dan (read: data that he has focused on). Dan notes that Gerry has applied certain filters when interpreting the data, which explains why Gerry sees Federer as numero uno.

Now Dan shows Gerry online statistics that indicate that both Federer and Agassi have the same winning rate in their careers on the court. He also shows Gerry web pages on Agassi's humanitarian achievements (read: data that he has focused on). Dan says that a tennis player, like any man, should be defined by his behavior on and off the court (read: assumptions). As such, he sees Agassi as the better tennis player (read: belief/interpretation based on meaning given to the data). Gerry now sees where Dan is coming from. Both are also a little less firm in their previous convictions on this subject, as they now understand that their opinions depend on the criteria each has applied to the definition of best tennis player of all time.

It is therefore important to take our counterparts down their "ladder of inference" through inquiry, before we take them up our own. However, without showing that we can be trusted and are able to empathize patiently with (without necessarily agreeing to) their perspectives, our counterparts may be reluctant to explain the data, interpretations and assumptions used to support their conclusions. Trust and empathy are thus key foundations for employing the "ladder of inference" (see Chapter 4 on building relationships). By understanding the significance and focus our counterparts place on their experiences and the information they have at hand, we can better explain why we have made different assumptions and interpretations from the available data. This can help in reducing their reactance to what we are saying, so we are in a better position to persuade them to draw a different conclusion from before. Understanding another's perspective and how they arrived at their views (again, without necessarily agreeing to their views) means a negotiator is less likely to reject her counterpart's view as nonsense, thereby mitigating the "us vs. them" mentality and reducing the barriers for both sides to come together.

Neutral mindset and being self-aware

It is important for a negotiator to be self-aware and attentive to her own mindset when preparing for and taking part in a negotiation. Distractions and biases can keep us from recognising potential allies and potential spoilers. Our preoccupations can also keep our minds from exploring potential solutions. This is similar to what some research has shown for situations in which a boss tends to criticise rather than encourage employees – it is not unusual for that boss's employees to be preoccupied with the negativity, thereby impairing their ability to think holistically and affecting their productivity at work! Self-awareness is also important so a negotiator knows her own set of interests, particularly which set is dominating in any given negotiation. By being aware, she can decide whether to "rein in" a particular interest or whether another set of interests should come out more strongly.

Example A: One of us moved to a new city only to find the store room in her new apartment locked by the landlord for his own storage. As the lease indicated she would be renting the whole apartment, she was frustrated but felt she could not do much since she was not familiar with local regulations and did not want to end up shopping for a new home (read: newbie mindset). After hearing about a friend's successful negotiation with his landlord, she realised her own fears had blocked her from thinking rationally through the options available. With a neutral mindset, she negotiated with the landlord and got a discount on her rent.

Example B: In a finance negotiation simulation, one of us received an instruction set focused on numeric data and costs. With her mind focused on the numbers, what she heard from her counterpart during the negotiation was interpreted through the "lens of numbers." As such, she kept trying to make the numbers add up rather than distill her counterpart's core interests. Instead of exploring a wide array of solutions, her proposed options were limited entirely to the "numbers radio frequency." Only later did she realize later that her counterpart was not at all interested in the numbers!

Example C: At one UN forum, one of us was invited to lunch by another negotiator who often played a spoiler role in the negotiations. Clouded by her own biases – more specifically, her inability to distinguish between the individual negotiator and his country's positions, she initially planned to decline the invitation. Thankfully, she accepted and got to learn more about the other negotiator – they have been friends ever since!

Personal views

In the course of UN negotiations, negotiators must sometimes debate issues about which they have strong personal views, which may or may not coincide with their country positions. A negotiator's first job is to promote her delegation's position while attempting to reach a compromise that can appeal to all delegations. As we have discussed, however, we hope that negotiators would also strive creatively, within this context, for good global outcomes. The definition of a good global outcome, however, may depend on your gender and country of origin. This is where it gets tricky, and can feel personal.

When another delegation's position is not only opposed to that of your delegation, but also the antithesis of your personal beliefs, it can be a difficult negotiation to maneuver. Subjects such as reproductive rights, women's rights, and human rights in general can fall into this category. In these cases, it is important to remain as unemotional as possible, to the point of appearing neutral. Try to remove the "self" from the discussion, promoting only your delegation's position with data and reasoned arguments. The other delegation's argument is likely not personal, and making it so will not help to demonstrate to the other party that their – or their delegation's or national – view is wrong. Your anger or emotion will evoke a response in your adversary: de-escalate, always.

Remember as well that some of these positions, as well as the personal views of negotiators, are often rooted in cultural norms and will be hard to combat directly. It is important to be sensitive to others' culturally-dictated behaviors and beliefs without compromising your own. Even personal space is cultural – what is legitimately friendly in one culture is offensive to another! One of us has gladly held hands working out compromises with certain African delegates, male and female, while standing respectfully away in discussions with Americans, Canadians, and some Asians.[8] Therefore, do not let your personal views color your reactions and response in negotiations, but keep your emotions in check and your responses sensitive.

Conclusion

Understanding interests – both your own and others – is the key to any effective and productive negotiation. An ability to decipher your counterpart's interests – and explain your own – using the "ladder of inference" tool is an important skill to develop, along with building trust and displaying empathy. In our experience, it is the rare negotiator who takes the time and opportunity to do this correctly (we have gotten it wrong ourselves) but more should take this approach. Finally, remember that a negotiation is precisely that. The point is to find options that can satisfy all parties' priority interests (remember lessons from Chapter 1). Focusing on "winning alone," without any sense of the cost to others, is a rookie's mistake and – if made repeatedly – can haunt a negotiator for the rest of her career in the UN.

Notes

1 Roger Fisher, Ury William, and Bruce Patton, *Getting to Yes: Negotiating Agreement without Giving In*, 2nd ed. (New York, N.Y.: Penguin Books, 1991).
2 *The Godfather*, directed by Francis Ford Coppola (1972; Hollywood, CA: Paramount Pictures and Alfran Productions, 2001), DVD.
3 Livni, Ephrat, "There's Only One Way to Truly Understand Another Person's Mind," *Quartz* (3 July 2018).
4 Eyal, Tal, Nicholas Epley, and Mary Steffel, "Perspective Mistaking: Accurately Understanding the Mind of Another Requires Getting Perspective, Not Taking Perspective," *Journal of Personality and Social Psychology*, Vol. 114, No. 4, (2018), 547.
5 Eyal, Tal, Nicholas Epley, and Mary Steffel, "Perspective Mistaking: Accurately Understanding the Mind of Another Requires Getting Perspective, Not Taking Perspective," *Journal of Personality and Social Psychology*, Vol. 114, No. 4, (2018), 568.
6 Livni, Ephrat, "There's Only One Way to Truly Understand Another Person's Mind," *Quartz* (3 July 2018).
7 This adaptation of the Ladder of Inference (C. Argyris) is used with permission of CMPartners LLC, 2018.
8 Amanda Erickson, "What 'Personal Space' Looks Like Around the World," *The Washington Post*, 24 April 2017.

Part Two

Inside the UN

3 The insider's guide to the UN negotiation system

In the movie Groundhog Day, Bill Murray finds himself in a time loop. He is extremely frustrated having to relive the same day over and over again. That is how some would describe life as a UN negotiator.

In your first year, you are excited about having a voice at the most representative negotiation table in the world. Admittedly, you find yourself slightly overwhelmed by the complex UN system, its rules of procedure and opaque negotiation process. You take heart that even those who speak seven languages fluently are flummoxed by "UNese," the UN's unique language. When family and friends ask about your work as a distinguished UN diplomat, you hesitate to reply – you have only just surfaced from the UN basement because the brightest minds could not agree whether to use "emphasizes" versus "stresses" in a UN resolution. The UN's punishing schedule leaves you with little time for the "real world." Nevertheless, you are determined to learn the ropes and conduct meaningful negotiations to make the world a better place!

Congrats! You are now in your second year. Wow, the discussions at the negotiation table sound so familiar. You can predict where this discussion is going to go. You jump in readily, trying to steer the debate to a better conclusion than last year's. Meanwhile, you may be facilitating (essentially chairing) a UN resolution, orchestrating the entire negotiation. It feels good when you deliver the baby. However, you can't help but wonder if local communities are actually going to benefit from these resolutions that contain your precious time, sweat, and tears. You also have tons of ideas on how the UN can improve – it is puzzling why no one implemented them before!

It is your third year at the UN. Now you know why those bright ideas didn't pass the finish line. Attempts to streamline the UN's work are jammed because no one wants to give up their pet issues. When you hear newbies proposing UN reform, you want to break the news to them gently, "that is not how the UN works." But that would mean zapping their idealism, which this organization ultimately requires.

You are even more aware of the continuous revolving UN door, with old allies being posted to new diplomatic assignments and noobs asking unanswered questions that have plagued your sleep for the last two years. There is no need for you to sit through the entire negotiation now as your established network will keep you updated. You can see the compromise outcome from miles away but know there is no point highlighting it too early. UN delegates will have to tire themselves out rehashing old arguments before they are willing to accept the compromise. The negotiation text continues to balloon – can these proposals even be implemented effectively to aid local communities or make positive change? That said, you are wise enough not to keep another negotiator from the satisfaction of having some of his proposals in the final text. Experience also tells you that agreement will not be reached unless every delegation is equally unhappy or indifferent. In any case, it is rare that anyone takes responsibility for failures in UN negotiations. It is usually some other delegation's fault.

If you are on your fourth or fifth year at the UN, you can't bring yourself to sit through the same negotiation for the umpteenth time. It is like a car wreck waiting to happen that you don't know how to stop. As such, you are either plotting your departure or finally enjoying the life New York City offers outside of 405 East 42nd Street!

Anonymous UN Diplomat

A negotiator must understand the system in which her negotiation takes place. This enables better decision-making and prevents unnecessary mistakes. For example, if you are looking to buy a carpet from Istanbul's Grand Bazaar, understanding the Grand Bazaar's haggling system dictates that you should arrive there at the start of the day, when salespersons are more eager to make a sale to reach their daily quota. Similarly, the above tongue-in-cheek description of life as a UN negotiator demonstrates the complex system in which UN negotiations operate.

This chapter details how negotiators can understand the system in which their negotiation is taking place. Looking at the UN, we demonstrate how negotiators identify (a) the key personalities involved in the negotiation; (b) the timeline for decision-making; and (c) the negotiation's history. The chapter also provides examples of the unique language and concepts used in UN negotiations.

Key personalities

It is useful for negotiators to chart the key personalities in their negotiation. Take the negotiations at the UN Framework Convention on Climate Change (UNFCCC) for example – there are 197 parties. Each party usually has several people in its delegation. There is also the UNFCCC Secretariat, which has a key role in supporting the work of the Member States. Additionally, there can be more than 30 draft decisions being negotiated at one time in the UNFCCC process. Mapping the key personalities can thus enable all the members in a delegation to be on the same page regarding the multiple moving pieces in the negotiations. It may also shed more light on particular negotiators.

Say you are negotiating draft decision 1 and Max from Country A has been giving you problems with his aggressive stance. Your colleague mentions that Max is negotiating draft decision 5 as well and has taken an aggressive position in that negotiation. Looking at the key personalities chart, your team notes that all the other Country A negotiators are very constructive in the negotiations for the other draft decisions. Ah! Could it be that Max is an aggressive negotiator and is taking a position far beyond the bottom-line in his brief? Or are draft decisions 1 and 5 more important to Country A than the other draft decisions on the table? Why is it in Max's interest to behave in this way in this negotiation process? Understanding such information helps you to know if there is room for Max to move his position in the negotiation.

Key personalities in a negotiation can include the chairperson, those who have the ear of the chairperson, those that have a key stake in the outcome (including people behind the scenes), moderates adept at bridging divides, those likely to dominate the negotiations, and potential spoilers (people who are determined to block agreement when they do not get their way). (See Chapter 4 for more on this.) Beware the spoiler who does not show up for most negotiation sessions, only to appear at the final round to block agreement!

With these key personalities in mind, a map of these personalities and the links between them (e.g. coalitions, hierarchical relationships, bad blood) can now be drawn up (Figure 3.1).

The map helps the negotiator keep track of all of the key personalities so she does not inadvertently miss out on consulting one of them during important intervals of the negotiation process. Checking in frequently with the various stakeholders gives the negotiator a sense of potential pitfalls ahead and helps her visualize who she should bring together for small group negotiations in an informal setting to make breakthroughs (as well as what coalitions she may need to block that might impede her ability to satisfy her interests). The map also identifies spoilers who block agreements just because they feel miffed about not being "sufficiently" consulted. Ultimately, the map reminds the negotiator to spend more time and effort consulting the top stakeholders. It also helps the negotiator to find a balanced solution by weighing the views of the various personalities accordingly. That said, it is just a tool to remember to reach out to the people involved; negotiators should remember that sometimes it only takes one spoiler to bring down a house of cards.

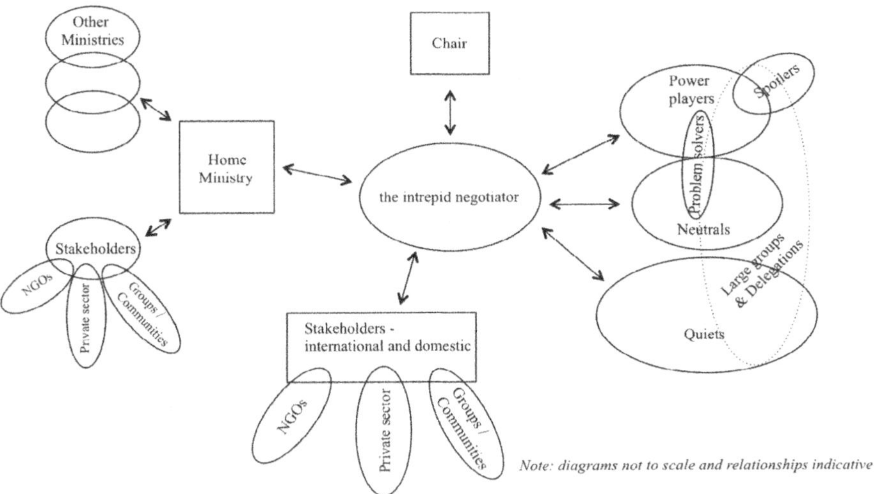

Figure 3.1 Key personalities map

Reading the room

Especially in informal negotiations (see Chapter 5), it is important to read the room during the first recitation of a proposed text and the first round of interventions. Who are the more vocal negotiators? Who is voicing support for each other's statements? Who is shaking her head or getting agitated when someone in particular speaks? Who do people seem to turn to for answers? This not only allows you to get to know the players and their prospective roles, it enables you to understand the dynamics between them. History between negotiators can alter how they behave in a given negotiation and these interactions impact the overall dynamic. Residual feelings from a previous negotiation – positive or negative – alter how certain delegates work together. This, of course, impacts you. Every negotiation – and every negotiated outcome, even on the same topic – is different every time, depending on who else is present.

Personal agendas

As a part of room reading, note behaviors, especially the actions of those you know. On some issues, some delegates have a personal agenda (remember different sets of interests in Chapter 2?). They may push more or less than their brief requires on a resolution about chocolate cake because they LOVE chocolate, and want it to be available everywhere. We don't promote this – everyone's agenda should be the best outcome for the world, within the framework of national instructions – but it is important to know that it is out there. In reading the room, try to perceive a delegate's real agenda. A good negotiator's personal views, including an understanding of the context of her negotiation, should influence how she presents and defends her national position; it should not change her national position.

Timeline for decision-making

In a negotiation, the timeline for making key decisions is based on two factors – hard deadlines (e.g. the non-negotiable date by when the agreement needs to be adopted) as well as the negotiation process. Returning to the example of the Grand Bazaar, you may find that the negotiation process there includes comparing prices at a few shops, making an opening bid, and being invited into the store for tea to haggle the final price. Not budgeting sufficient time for comparing prices at a few stores in your timeline could thus affect the final price on which you agree for your purchase.

At the UN, consultations on a draft resolution often take place with key stakeholders even before the draft is formally presented to the wider UN membership. This is because negotiators dislike being caught unprepared in a formal negotiation; when caught by surprise, some become defensive and object excessively, regardless of the merits of the proposal. It is therefore important to factor sufficient consultation time into the timeline for decision-making. This applies to negotiations outside the UN as well.

After the draft resolution has been introduced at a formal UN meeting, the proponents continue canvassing for support for their proposal. They engage delegations that have objections and counter-proposals. From these consultations, the proponents make amendments, negotiate further with their respective home agencies, and convene more meetings to iron out differences. Only then is the resolution ready for adoption. To understand the negotiation system in which one is operating, including the timeline for decision-making, one must thus spend time learning about the negotiation process for similar negotiations.

Take the simple example of Lin's birthday party, the timeline for her decision-making may simply consist of the following – when to send out the invites to friends, when to prepare the party food and drinks, when to serve the various courses of dinner during the party, and when to call it a night. In a complex negotiation, however, the timeline can be significantly more intricate. In such cases, it is useful to chart out key dates in the negotiation process to help keep track of prime opportunities for persuasion and gathering information.

As a case in point, each September at the UN, the Chair of the G77 and China looks for negotiators to represent the group on the various resolutions

UN RESOLUTION NEGOTIATION TIMELINE

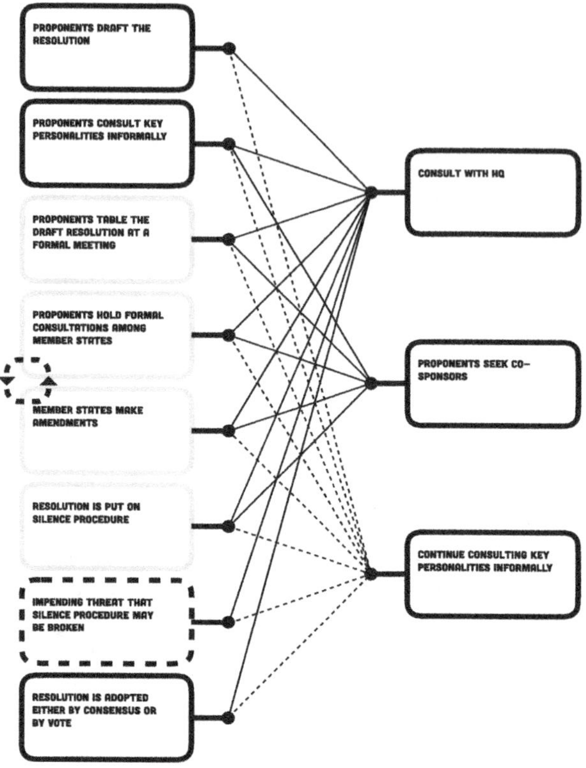

Note: diagrams not to scale and relationships indicative

Figure 3.2 UN resolution negotiation timeline

that will be negotiated in the General Assembly that fall. (The "G77[1] and China" is the largest negotiating bloc at the UN as it represents the interests of over 130 developing countries, spanning St Kitts & Nevis to Singapore to South Africa.) The Bureaus of the six UN committees also look for facilitators to chair these negotiations. This period is thus a prime opening for UN negotiators to get clued in on new resolutions that will be tabled that fall and their potential challenges. It is an opportunity to influence the draft resolutions before they are tabled in formal UN meetings. Those wanting to facilitate (i.e. chair) a resolution can also get the pick of the crop at this time.

Apart from key dates, such as when the first draft agreement should be tabled, the timeline for decision-making should also reflect any long periods during which key personalities are likely to be unavailable for negotiations. When Singapore and Luxembourg co-chaired the UN negotiations for the "Five Year Review of the Mauritius Strategy of Implementation" in the month of June, they knew the final agreement had to be submitted to the

General Assembly by that September. They were also aware that most negotiators would be away in August. This departure would have a massive impact on the momentum of the negotiations as some negotiators may return in September, wanting to unravel agreements reached in the draft before the summer holiday, while others may have forgotten the compromises that had been made thus far in the negotiations and try to play hardball. The co-chairs therefore made it clear to the negotiators that the negotiations would close by the end of July. This sent a clear signal to all involved that there was no time for delay tactics and other negotiation games. Due to the co-chairs' strong grasp of the negotiation system and timeline, they were able to effectively and efficiently shepherd the UN Member States to a good agreement in just a few weeks.

Negotiation history

When the scar on Harry Potter's head starts to hurt him, we get the sense that Voldemort may be up to some big bad scheme because we know the history between Potter's scar and Voldemort's actions. At the UN, we can tell a lot about what is happening – and what will likely happen – in a negotiation from its negotiation history. For example, history tells us that when a small group of countries request recognition for their unique circumstance and need for more financial resources in a UN resolution, other groups of countries will likely request similar recognition and resources.

Before diving into a negotiation, look at its history – it can provide explanations on why delegations act as they currently do. It can give a negotiator insight into what another delegation's next move might be. It can also suggest ways to resolve deadlocks similar to those faced in the past and can provide a heads-up on potential problems. Look as well at related negotiations and their outcomes to get an idea of "precedence."

Concepts

A negotiator should familiarize herself with historical concepts and phrases used in the negotiation – precedence. One such concept to understand at the UN is "silence procedure." Negotiations on a resolution continue until the chairperson believes the draft text balances the needs of all the key parties and has a high chance of adoption. At this point, the chairperson places the draft under "silence procedure" for about 24 hours. This gives negotiators time to reconfirm with their headquarters that they can accept the draft. If no amendments are proposed during this period, the text is understood to be acceptable to all parties and ready for adoption. Breaking silence procedure is a highly controversial move and not looked upon favorably. Chairpersons have therefore used silence procedure to push through closure of a draft resolution in extremely tough negotiations, where the draft has likely reached its ultimate balance, but the parties are unwilling to acknowledge this publicly.

Another historical concept used in UN and other multilateral negotiations is "nothing is agreed until everything is agreed." When a paragraph in the draft resolution has been "cleaned" of amendments (i.e. the negotiators appear to have reached agreement on the paragraph), the chairperson can "close" the paragraph to further edits by designating it as "agreed ad ref."[2] Reopening an "agreed ad ref" paragraph is generally frowned on. The resolution, however, can only be adopted when every paragraph in the draft is "agreed ad ref." This means that, if the negotiations conclude with no agreement over just one paragraph, all the other "agreed ad ref" paragraphs are considered null and void. This was the case in the 19th session of the Commission on Sustainable Development (CSD19) in 2011. After weeks of intense negotiations, negotiators successfully reached agreement on improving the sustainability of the transport and mining sectors, as well as on the 10-Year Framework of Programmes on Sustainable Consumption and Production Patterns – all substantively difficult achievements. Unfortunately, negotiations broke down on a paragraph concerning the rights of people in occupied territories in another section of the outcome document. As a result, all agreements negotiated at CSD19 were considered null and void.

UN venues

The UN consists of a variety of bodies (see UN System diagram, Figure 3.3).[3] This book focuses mainly on the negotiation context for the UN General Assembly in New York, which is often applicable as well to the UN Funds and Programmes, and many of the multilateral environmental agreements (collectively the venues with which we are most familiar). UN Headquarters exist in New York and Geneva and there are large UN offices in Nairobi, Vienna, and Rome, with smaller UN offices, or specific body headquarters, in other cities across the globe.

It is important to note that each forum – and every UN location – has its own negotiation history, dynamics, and atmospherics. Often, the organs of the UN General Assembly and the Economic and Social Council function similarly, in terms of process and protocol. Varying memberships in each body alter the dynamics to some extent. The Specialized Agencies, such as the World Intellectual Property Organization and the International Civil Aviation Organization, each have their own rules and procedures, which can translate into drastically different processes, and their dynamics often vary significantly from those of the UN in New York. The Security Council, due to its very limited membership and binding decisions, is even more distinct.

To be most effective, a negotiator should familiarize herself with the history, rules, and atmospherics of each venue in advance of any negotiation. Tactics that work well in aggressive New York negotiations, for example, may not translate well into other fora. For more details on UN forums, we recommend Linda M. Fasulo's "An Insider's Guide to the UN," the UN's

"Basic Facts about the UN," and the UN Handbook (published annually by New Zealand's Ministry of Foreign Affairs and Trade).[4]

UN General Assembly Main Committees

As we refer to some of the General Assembly's Main Committees in this book, the list of committees is below.

- First Committee: disarmament and international security matters.
- Second Committee: economic and financial issues.
- Third Committee: social, humanitarian and cultural issues.
- Fourth Committee: special political and decolonization matters.
- Fifth Committee: administrative and budgetary items.
- Sixth Committee: legal matters.

Word play

Code words are scattered throughout UN texts; clues to the true purpose – or intent – of such words can often be found in the history of a negotiation. Some code words help obscure, contributing to vague language (see below); others actually clarify. Regardless, it is important to look out for strange vocabulary or anomalous usage, because there may be a double meaning. Words like "inter alia" and "such as" are exceedingly useful to avoid listing everything under the sun that is important to each delegation. For example, "we recognize the importance of, inter alia, flour in making chocolate chip cookies." Without "inter alia," we might also need to list a number of ingredients, some of which may be up for debate (white sugar or brown sugar, butter or margarine, baking powder or soda…).

Another code phrase is "technology transfer," which is an implicit reference to provisions in the WTO agreement on trade-related aspects of intellectual property rights (TRIPS) regarding incentives for developed country industries to share technological innovations with least developed countries. That phrase is often qualified by the phrase "as mutually agreed," which is intended to make explicit that such transfers must be agreed with the holders of the relevant intellectual property rights. Other code words notably, "within existing resources" and "with extrabudgetary resources," among others ("among others" is another nice phrase like "inter alia"), speak to financial commitments. These two phrases, respectively, say that the Secretariat may not seek new resources, and that additional donations will be needed to implement the actions under discussion.

The history of a negotiation can also help identify likely "trigger words." These are words that have a contentious history in the negotiation. One example at the UN is "human security," which may seem straightforward literally, but is a hotly debated subject. The visceral response from some countries to its mere mention can thus throw off the newbie who raised it unknowingly. Another example is the concept of "common but differentiated responsibilities,"

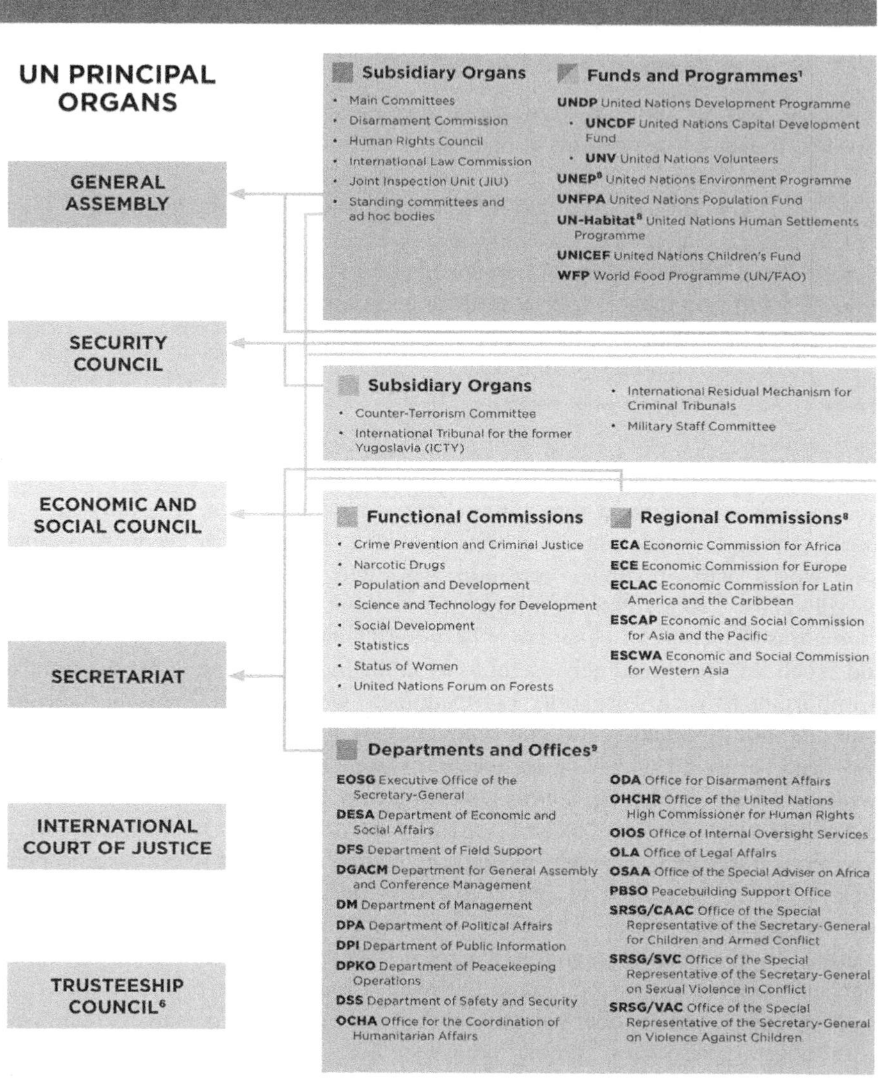

Figure 3.3 UN system chart

The United Nations System

Research and Training

UNIDIR United Nations Institute for Disarmament Research

UNITAR United Nations Institute for Training and Research

UNSSC United Nations System Staff College

UNU United Nations University

Other Entities

ITC International Trade Centre (UN/WTO)

UNCTAD[1,8] United Nations Conference on Trade and Development

UNHCR[1] Office of the United Nations High Commissioner for Refugees

UNOPS[1] United Nations Office for Project Services

UNRWA[1] United Nations Relief and Works Agency for Palestine Refugees in the Near East

UN-Women[1] United Nations Entity for Gender Equality and the Empowerment of Women

Related Organizations

CTBTO Preparatory Commission Preparatory Commission for the Comprehensive Nuclear-Test-Ban Treaty Organization

IAEA[1,3] International Atomic Energy Agency

ICC International Criminal Court

IOM[1] International Organization for Migration

ISA International Seabed Authority

ITLOS International Tribunal for the Law of the Sea

OPCW[3] Organization for the Prohibition of Chemical Weapons

WTO[1,4] World Trade Organization

- Peacekeeping operations and political missions
- Sanctions committees (ad hoc)
- Standing committees and ad hoc bodies

Peacebuilding Commission

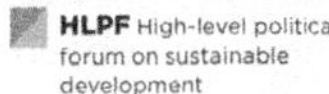

HLPF High-level political forum on sustainable development

Other Bodies

- Committee for Development Policy
- Committee of Experts on Public Administration
- Committee on Non-Governmental Organizations
- Permanent Forum on Indigenous Issues

UNAIDS Joint United Nations Programme on HIV/AIDS

UNGEGN United Nations Group of Experts on Geographical Names

Research and Training

UNICRI United Nations Interregional Crime and Justice Research Institute

UNRISD United Nations Research Institute for Social Development

UNISDR United Nations Office for Disaster Risk Reduction

UNODC[1] United Nations Office on Drugs and Crime

UNOG United Nations Office at Geneva

UN-OHRLLS Office of the High Representative for the Least Developed Countries, Landlocked Developing Countries and Small Island Developing States

UNON United Nations Office at Nairobi

UNOP[2] United Nations Office for Partnerships

UNOV United Nations Office at Vienna

Specialized Agencies[1,5]

FAO Food and Agriculture Organization of the United Nations

ICAO International Civil Aviation Organization

IFAD International Fund for Agricultural Development

ILO International Labour Organization

IMF International Monetary Fund

IMO International Maritime Organization

ITU International Telecommunication Union

UNESCO United Nations Educational, Scientific and Cultural Organization

UNIDO United Nations Industrial Development Organization

UNWTO World Tourism Organization

UPU Universal Postal Union

WHO World Health Organization

WIPO World Intellectual Property Organization

WMO World Meteorological Organization

WORLD BANK GROUP[7]

- **IBRD** International Bank for Reconstruction and Development
- **IDA** International Development Association
- **IFC** International Finance Corporation

Notes:

1 Members of the United Nations System Chief Executives Board for Coordination (CEB).
2 UN Office for Partnerships (UNOP) is the UN's focal point vis-a-vis the United Nations Foundation, Inc.
3 IAEA and OPCW report to the Security Council and the General Assembly (GA).
4 WTO has no reporting obligation to the GA, but contributes on an ad hoc basis to GA and Economic and Social Council (ECOSOC) work on, inter alia, finance and development issues.
5 Specialized agencies are autonomous organizations whose work is coordinated through ECOSOC (intergovernmental level) and CEB (inter-secretariat level).
6 The Trusteeship Council suspended operation on 1 November 1994, as on 1 October 1994 Palau, the last United Nations Trust Territory, became independent.
7 International Centre for Settlement of Investment Disputes (ICSID) and Multilateral Investment Guarantee Agency (MIGA) are not specialized agencies in accordance with Articles 57 and 63 of the Charter, but are part of the World Bank Group.
8 The secretariats of these organs are part of the UN Secretariat.
9 The Secretariat also includes the following offices: The Ethics Office, United Nations Ombudsman and Mediation Services, Office of Administration of Justice and the Office on Sport for Development and Peace

This Chart is a reflection of the functional organization of the United Nations System and for informational purposes only. It does not include all offices or entities of the United Nations System.

Published by the United Nations Department of Public Information DPI/2470 rev.5 —17-00023— March 2017 which may seem innocuous to the layman, but is bound to result in fireworks in UN negotiations because of its history in certain arenas where it has been interpreted to mean that developed countries should do more than developing countries.

Scheduling

Understanding negotiation history also helps one appreciate the workload of fellow negotiators so that approaches can be better strategized. The teenager who wants to negotiate for more pocket money may be more successful approaching his relaxed parents over the weekend than on a Wednesday, when they are stressed out from work. For the UN, the third week of September until the end of December is when the General Assembly negotiates and adopts most of its annual resolutions. A UN negotiator may thus be preoccupied with over ten resolutions at this time. With so many competing priorities, allies in one's negotiation may fail to attend an important session. Knowing this, one may need to send them reminders so they show up in full force to speak up for one's proposal. Alternatively, one can try to schedule a negotiation session for 9am. Negotiation sessions tend to overlap during the busiest period of 10am-6pm. An early start thus means fewer competing meetings at the same time. Negotiators also do not turn up early at the UN unless something important is at stake. A 9am session therefore weeds out potential spoilers who "drop by" negotiations without having done their homework, tabling proposals or asking questions that sidetrack the discussion.

Disagreements

A negotiation's history can also provide tips on resolving disagreements. For UN resolutions, there are three main ways to resolve a paragraph under negotiation. The first replaces the text in dispute with "agreed language," which is text from previously adopted resolutions. The upside of agreed language is that it avoids repeated fights that are unlikely to reach a better conclusion than before. The downside is that the "agreed language" could be taken out of context, rendering the text meaningless. Worse still, it could convey or perpetuate something completely unintended.

The second way to paper over differences is the all-or-nothing approach. This is done by including or deleting all of the proposals on the divisive issue. The problem with the include-all approach is that it can result in a convoluted document that no one ultimately understands and which is difficult or impossible to implement. On the other hand, some negotiators try to invoke the delete-all approach to remove a paragraph or idea they do not like, but for which they do not have a good argument to simply call for its removal. To do this, they add extreme text (a poison pill) that they know will never be accepted by another party (or all other parties). The goal is to provoke others to call for the deletion of the entire section to break the stalemate.

A third way to resolve a disputed paragraph is through constructive ambiguity. This means using vague language that can be interpreted differently to meet the various parties' bottom-lines. Take the dad who announces to his family that, "We are going on holiday." The son starts researching what country the family should travel to. The daughter envisions her wardrobe for the family drive to the beach. The dad, who meant that he and his wife will be taking the day off tomorrow, is pleasantly surprised that the rest of the family is in such good spirits too! There will be subsequent chaos, but for now, everyone is happy. Likewise, when using constructive ambiguity at the UN, problems arise during the implementation phase.

Although valuable in difficult situations where an agreement is politically necessary, these approaches should be used judiciously, so as not to perpetuate agreements that have minimal value.

Conclusion

Understanding the chronology, history, and characters in a story helps to navigate the storyline when reading a book. Similarly, when navigating a negotiation, it is useful to identify the timeline for decision-making, the key personalities involved, and the negotiation's history. (After all, virtually every UN General Assembly negotiation is a sequel!) Doing so provides signals and insights that can guide your words and actions towards a successful negotiated outcome.

More tips for those working with UN resolutions for the first time:

A practical guide to outcome documents[5]

By Ye-Min Wu and Benito Jiménez Sauma
At the time of publication, Benito Jiménez Sauma is the Alternate Permanent Representative at the Permanent Mission of Mexico to the United Nations Rome-based Agencies.

Introduction

The official outcome of committees of the UN General Assembly, and other main organs of the UN, take the form of "Resolutions" – official documents adopted by the UN membership to address a particular issue. Negotiating resolutions, particularly during the General Assembly session, is the main activity of delegates.

To the new delegate, these pieces of text might look odd, with peculiar English grammar – neither American nor from the United Kingdom, and written in a rigid way. It can take some time to grasp the logic and peculiarities of the language used for UN resolutions. This article tries to help readers better understand their logic as well as how delegates play with the language contained in them to further their respective interests.

Process

Most General Assembly resolutions are recurring; i.e. when a draft resolution is "first" presented, it is most likely based on the previous resolution on the same subject, with appropriate updates. (This can be a problem when recurring resolutions are not "retired" but rehashed with little value added.)

Every Committee of the General Assembly has traditional rules of work. For example, most sustainable development resolutions in the Second Committee (2C) are proposed by the G-77 and China; other resolutions in the Committee are presented by individual countries or by a group of sponsor countries. Additionally, 2C "operates by consensus," meaning that voting on resolutions is discouraged and delegates do their best to achieve outcomes that can be adopted by "consensus." Resolutions adopted by consensus (instead of a vote) can be said to have more legitimacy and hold wider support. The downside is that consensus resolutions are likely to be more watered down, as language acceptable to all parties (i.e. the lowest common denominator) is necessary to achieve consensus. Negotiations may also last longer since parties with differing views from the sponsors may have less incentive to shift their position since the onus is on the sponsors to achieve a consensus resolution.

Once a draft resolution is presented, it requires intensive labor to be adopted. The actions include: circulating the draft on time to all delegations; explaining to delegations what the proponents want to say via their resolution; canvassing for support and engaging with delegations that don't share the proponents' point of view; accepting amendments – friendly or unfriendly; convening formal and informal meetings to iron out differences and discuss ideas; crafting compromises; and finally, adopting the resolution in the Committee and then the General Assembly itself. There are any number of meetings that take place, official and otherwise, about a resolution before it gets to the adoption stage; this takes extensive time.

After delegates appear to reach agreement on a resolution, or when the sponsors of the resolution decide to close the text, it is placed under the "silence procedure" before being sent to the UN secretariat in preparation for its adoption. Silence procedure typically lasts for 24 hours and is an opportunity for delegates to confirm with their Headquarters that the final text is acceptable. A silence procedure is rarely broken; doing so is considered a dramatic move with potentially significant implications for an eventual agreement.

Structure of resolutions

A UN resolution is composed of articles in two sections, the preambular section followed by the operative section. The preambular section describes the recent history and some elements of the current situation of the topic under consideration. It will likely include references to previous resolutions adopted on the same topic. Preambular paragraphs usually begin with a verb in the present-participle form, to describe an ongoing situation (past and current).

The operative section focuses on recommendations to address the issue at hand. These paragraphs begin with a verb in the third person, present-singular form. The recommendations contained in operative paragraphs could be addressed to UN Member States, the UN secretariat, or other stakeholders outside the UN. General Assembly resolutions, unlike those issued by the Security Council, are non-binding. Its spirit is that they have to be followed. Nevertheless, this means it is difficult to enforce compliance of General Assembly resolutions for Member States and stakeholders; however, recommendations related to the UN secretariat are interpreted as mandates by UN staff.

There is no limit on the number of preambular or operative paragraphs a resolution can have. Some resolutions have more preambular paragraphs than operative paragraphs, and vice-versa. Some resolutions are so long they lose their readers and, more importantly, their impact mid-way. (Negotiating note: when a delegate proposes to "streamline" a draft to make it "concise," it may be with a view to making it comprehensible or – more likely – an excuse to remove proposals that are unacceptable to the delegate.) Other delegates, without clearing away the cobwebs, simply pile additional text into a previous resolution. This can result in redundant language in the latest resolution.

Take for example the UN resolution on Agenda 21, otherwise known as "Implementation of Agenda 21, the Programme for the Further Implementation of Agenda 21 and the outcomes of the World Summit on Sustainable Development." Due to a lack of spring cleaning over the years, by the 65th session of the General Assembly, this resolution had chalked up a page's worth of preambular paragraphs, many of which simply recalled previous UN resolutions. Thankfully, delegates negotiating this resolution for the 66th session agreed to trim these to just two paragraphs.

Legally, language in operative sections is stronger in significance than preambular language. Delegates wanting to send a strong message on an issue should thus focus on the operative section. (Negotiating note: A common tactic to "water down" an issue, or to solve a fundamental divergence of views, is to move proposed text from the operative section to the preambular section.)

The general format of a resolution is as follows:

- Paragraphs are single-spaced, separated by two spaces.
- Paragraphs start with a verb phrase in italics (present-participle for preambular or third person, present-singular for operative).
- Preambular paragraphs end with commas.
- Operative paragraphs end with semi-colons.

- Preambular paragraphs are not numbered in the final text, but during negotiations are referred to as "preambular paragraph one," "preambular paragraph two," etc., written in the text as "pp1, pp2," etc.
- Operative paragraphs are numbered in the final text with Arabic numbers, and are referred to during negotiations as "operative paragraph one," "operative paragraph two," etc., and written in the text as "OP1, OP2," etc.
- There is only one period in the whole text and it is located at the end of the last operative paragraph.

Language

A resolution conveys messages through its language: the preambular section serves to present a diagnosis of the issue, and the operative section the actions to address it. The nuances in the language at the beginning of each paragraph reflect different degrees of preoccupation, importance, or urgency regarding the subject at hand.

For example, in the operative section, where the recommendations are made, "endorses" is one of the strongest verbs that can be used. This is followed by "welcomes." "Notes" or "takes note" are less forceful – they are useful for papering over differences of opinion among delegations, and can be used to point out that an item (e.g. document or event) exists without expressing an opinion on the subject. "Takes note with satisfaction ..." is stronger than "takes note with appreciation ...," which is stronger than "takes note with interest ..." On the negative side, "takes note with preoccupation" sends a less somber message than "takes note with concern" or "notes with regret."

You would be surprised at the amount of time delegates can spend trying to find agreement between just a few words, like "Notes" and "Recognizes," or even on the placement of a comma (such "little" shifts can change all the meaning)!

Examples of preambular phrases are:

Conscious of ...
Emphasizing ...
Expressing deep concern ...
Noting/Noting also/Noting further ...
Noting with concern ...
Reaffirming ...
Recalling ...
Recognizing/Recognizing also/Recognizing further ...
Reiterating ...
Reiterating its deep concern ...
Reiterating its serious concern ...

Examples of operative verbs are:

Acknowledges
Appeals
Approves
Calls for
Calls upon
Commends/Also commends
Decides/Also decides
Emphasizes
Encourages
Endorses
Expresses concern
Expresses its appreciation
Expresses its firm conviction
Expresses serious concern
Invites
Notes
Reaffirms/Also reaffirms/Reaffirms further
Recalls
Recognizes/Also recognizes/Recognizes further
Reiterates
Requests/Also requests
Stresses
Takes note
Takes note with appreciation
Takes note with interest
Takes note with preoccupation
Takes note with regret
Takes note with satisfaction
Urges
Welcomes/Also welcomes

Turns of phrase

Delegates use a variety of options to paper over disagreements during a negotiation, with a view to closing pending paragraphs and getting to agreement. Most often, these tactics are employed by chairs who have their eyes on the clock, or calendar. These options include, inter alia (another common term), "agreed language," removal of a concept entirely, and vague language.

The use of "agreed language" involves recycling language on a subject from a previous resolution, this is also called "previously agreed" language. This is sometimes the best thing to do when delegates cannot agree on a proposed paragraph, but it has the downside of again rehashing the same ideas. The rationale behind using agreed language is that the text or paragraph was previously agreed by UN Member States and should therefore not be a problem for the current negotiation, especially since the parties are the same. It additionally avoids repetitive arguments over a longstanding issue and can help mask the fact that delegations may not be experts in the issues at stake. The disadvantage is that the text chosen can be taken out of its original context and, as a result, it loses its meaning or connotes something quite different in the current draft resolution than originally intended. When discussing agreed language, delegates will often insist that it be "verbatim" for this reason; however, context is often still lost.

Another other option is to "cancel out" the various parties' proposals on the divisive issue. This can be done by deleting all the proposals related to the contentious issue, whether or not inclusion of the issue was even necessary to begin with. This has the benefits of shortening the text and removing potentially meaningless language. The downside, of course, is that the issue (if important) is not included.

A third option is to use vague language that makes everyone happy (or really equally upset) due to its ambiguity. Sometimes such language is called "constructive ambiguity" and is verbiage that can be interpreted differently depending on each party's interest, often in order to disguise the fact that delegates were unable to resolve an issue. Constructive ambiguity may also purposely distort grammar rules, for example omitting articles or using verbs incorrectly, in order to achieve the appropriate level of vagueness.

Ideally, language in a resolution should be clear and precise, so that it can be understood by everyone, especially those who will need to implement it. Unfortunately, this is not always the case, as it is not always the means to achieve compromise at the UN.

Other items

When drafting operative paragraphs, one should also be realistic about what is achievable, including checking if the resolution will have financial implications. In general, a resolution that has financial implications not covered in the current UN budget can face more difficulties with adoption.

We have discussed "resolutions" but there is another type of formal action taken by UN bodies. They are called "decisions." Decisions have less legal force than resolutions and they generally concern procedural matters, such as elections, appointments, time and place of future sessions. It is rare for some Committees, like the Second Committee, to deal with decisions. However, they may be used as a last-resort, when fundamental divisions on the subject at hand remain and the Membership basically wants to keep the issue on the agenda for the next session. (Negotiating note: process and procedural resolutions – or decisions – can sometimes be the most difficult to negotiate; in the UN, process is king.) Additionally, depending on the venue, there are "outcome documents," "declarations," "accords," "statements," "international agreements," and treaties, among others.

Conclusion

Drafting resolutions at the UN requires some basic expertise in the English language and in negotiation, but these are not difficult skills to learn. Delegates, regardless of their stand on the issue, as well as the secretariat, are often happy to answer questions; we caution newbies, however, to also consider motives in taking advice. While this article is an abbreviated introduction to drafting resolutions, the UN Institute for Training and Research (UNITAR) offers more detailed courses on drafting UN resolutions that could be useful for delegates.

General Assembly resolutions help guide UN policies. They also send a signal to the world on that particular subject. Since negotiations for a resolution involve the whole UN Membership, one must take into account the various points of view to adopt the resolution. For this, delegates use creative ways to draft text to get the approval of the general Membership. That said, the language of a resolution should be clear and concise so that all can understand and implement the resolution accordingly. If resolutions do not effectively address the problems at hand, it can lead to the marginalization of the UN.

Notes

1 The G77 stands for the Group of 77, even though the Group now represents more than 77 countries. The "official" count as of publication is 134.
2 "Ref" is short for referendum.
3 From the UN Department of Information, Copyright 2017 United Nations. Reprinted with the permission of the United Nations. Last modified March 13, 2017. Accessed May 23, 2018. http://www.un.org/en/aboutun/structure/pdfs/UN%20System%20Chart_ENG_FINAL_MARCH13_2017.pdf
4 Linda M. Fasulo, *An Insider's Guide to the UN* (New Haven: Yale University Press, 2004). UN, *Basic Facts about the United Nations 42nd Edition* (New York: UN, 2017) – also available online. The UN Handbook by New Zealand's Ministry of Foreign Affairs and Trade is also available as an app (#UNHandbookApp).
5 With permission from Benito Jiménez Sauma.

4 Don't go it alone: Building relationships and alliances

At the UN, it literally "takes a village" or, at the very least, a co-conspirator, for a negotiator to achieve her goals. To successfully put together a proposal, forge agreement, or even block an outcome, a negotiator must work with others. This is not only because delegates usually solve the hard parts of a negotiation in backroom deals and via side schemes, but because the give and take of formal negotiations, including the staged pageantry necessary to formalize and socialize the outcome of an informal process, depend on understandings between delegates (see more on backroom deals in Chapter 5). To play a real part in shaping the outcome, one must be included in these side schemes or backroom processes, either by invitation or as a convener, and able to effectively communicate across the table. Both require the building of relationships and alliances.

This chapter looks at the essential categories of relationships a negotiator will confront (and should court) and delves into how alliances are built. It also proposes some tips that negotiators can add to their networking toolkit to strengthen these relationships. The chapter closes with a discussion of groups, a particular sort of alliance at the UN.

Relationships

Regardless of the merit of a proposal in a UN negotiation (be it a new initiative or a solution to an existing issue), delegations may resist it – or even block it – because of its proponent. If the negotiator putting forward the proposal is disliked or not respected, the proposal is probably dead in the water. A proposal is likely to meet the same fate if it comes from the "wrong" delegation (more on this later) or an unknown delegate. Further complicating matters, seasoned UN negotiators tend to look suspiciously at proposals from new negotiators in general, such that any truly original proposal is guilty of "interference" until proven innocent.

The ability of a negotiator to effectively achieve her goals through creativity and compromise thus greatly depends on her rapport with others (remember Chapter 3 on key personalities). If the rapport is good, she is more likely to get help when in a bind or receive some latitude when she has to promote an unpopular position. Examples from our own experience include: another delegate being willing to voice our delegation's positions at meetings when we were unable to attend; delegations helping to delay decisions on issues of interest to our delegation when we needed more time; and delegates from delegations with opposing views offering to find a solution with us before the formal meeting, even when they knew the deck was stacked against us. Clearly, a successful negotiator needs to harness the power of relationships. And, as with most interactions, it is helpful to cultivate a persona that is likeable and respected by demonstrating warmth and at least some level of competence (though there are exceptions to this for one-off negotiations or truly difficult players).

There are a variety of delegates a negotiator will encounter and therefore a variety of relationships that she should cultivate. At the risk of over-generalising, we have categorised the most essential under: *friendlies* (delegations with similar views); *opposites* (delegations with differing views); *key personalities* (which include *power players, problem solvers, and spoilers*); and *quiets and neutrals* (often, the majority). The categories are not mutually exclusive. For example, an *opposite* in negotiation A may be a *friendly* in negotiation B; an *opposite* may also be a *key personality*. Each of these broad categories of people benefits from a specialised approach to relationship building. And of course, the most successful negotiators attempt to build relationships with everyone.

Friendlies

The easiest relationships to develop are often between negotiators from delegations with common or similar positions. These people will be inclined to not just build a relationship with you but be an immediate ally (just don't mess it up, which is as good as losing your ammunition in reserve!). They are more likely to trust you than other negotiators.

Begin over coffee, before a negotiation if possible, gathering advice and discussing approaches to achieve common aims; discuss tag teaming common problems (joining voices or speaking from different perspectives to the same end), piling on each other's formal statements to cement positions (underlining arguments or highlighting different components of an argument in independent interventions), and dividing the labor (e.g. sharing the load by assigning each delegation an *opposite* for targeted outreach or one piece of a joint problem on which to focus). If you have built the relationship, you may find that negotiators in this category are more willing to fight your battles for you. You may also wish to pay it forward subsequently by mentoring new negotiators in this category, given that you probably share common goals and could use some strong backers in the field.

Due to the ease of building relationships among *friendlies*, negotiators new to a forum often begin relationship-building in this category (it makes perfect sense and it is easier). The risk, however, is getting stuck working only with this group without venturing beyond, to build relationships elsewhere (especially with the *opposites*). This is bad practice that has implications for the potential of a successful outcome. Fraternizing only with a limited, similar group restricts a negotiator's understanding of the scope of the negotiation and the other delegates, as well as confining the space for creative ideas for compromise. Any outcome, by necessity, includes the agreement of a group larger than your own *friendlies*. It can also result in a type of group think, causing these negotiators to believe more fervently that they are right and anyone not in their camp is wrong, which makes compromise more difficult.

Opposites

These can be the trickiest relationships to build, but once formed, they can be the strongest and most important. After all, negotiations are about bridging divides and working closely with those who do not share your view in order to find solutions acceptable to the various parties. When meeting an *opposite* for the first time, expect her guard to be up, and for her to view your ideas with some suspicion or skepticism. Due to this high level of reactance, *opposites* will be unlikely to be readily inclined to forge a relationship, much less an alliance.

To break through the mistrust, start with humility. Humility is not weakness; it is accepting that we don't have all the answers and should be willing to listen to what others have to say on a subject. Also, avoid "showboating" – no one likes a "know-it-all" or to be made to feel inferior. To build trust, take the time to get to know an *opposite* as a human being and for them to understand you as one. You can start by offering to have coffee and, if they accept, remember to talk less and listen more. If possible, invite them to meet outside the formal working environment (off campus), or even to your home and to meet your family, so they see there is a "real" you. Let your hair down together through karaoke or sporting activities (we note that karaoke has been very popular and effective among New York delegates, and that even negotiators

involved in contentious climate change negotiations go out for drinks afterwards). This helps both sides to distinguish between the person and her flag, and especially between the individual and the positions for which she is advocating. Once some trust has been established, you can continue to build confidence and goodwill by quietly proposing solutions to problems an *opposite* faces on the sidelines of a negotiation and really hearing the other's response and concerns. Over time and with conscious investment in the relationship, these *opposites* can almost become allies.

Key personalities (power players, problem solvers, and spoilers)

As in any new job, getting to know the *power players* is helpful to success. These individuals will be evident after your observation of the first few meetings (see Chapters 3 and 5 for additional information) – they will dominate the discussion either at the microphone or behind the scenes. Often, the *power players* are from a larger delegation or group; at other times, it is about their strong personalities. These are the negotiators who – for good or ill – dominate the process. With many people (and issues) trying to get their attention, the *power players* have to prioritize their time and resources. Show them you are an effective negotiator and can be useful in carrying the water on mutual interests or by solving their problems. Demonstrate to them that you will stand firm when your interests are at stake. Overall, make an impact on them.

For example, at an Ambassadorial-level meeting on climate change, an Ambassador who was new to the forum publically took a *power player* to task for calling on other countries to do more to address climate change when the latter's country was not seen to be doing enough. After the meeting, several other *power players* came up to introduce themselves to the new Ambassador. In this case, the play worked, and the new Ambassador got the attention of some key players; this was, however, a bold move that could have backfired. The *power players* can help you immensely if they are on your side. They can also harm you if they aren't, particularly if they deem you a walkover – or worse, useless.

Likewise, the *problem solvers* are always good to know and appreciate. These individuals want to help everyone to get to a mutually satisfying outcome, as efficiently as possible, with as few perceived losses. They likely have their own goals as well, but their overarching motivation is often to get to the best outcome for all (we would encourage every negotiator to consider this a goal!). If the *problem solvers* are on your side, your key needs will be protected. You will recognize them by their behaviors: scurrying around the room, or actively communicating on WhatsApp, talking to everyone, and huddling with a wide variety of delegations. They are always present in – and often the conveners of – side schemes and backroom discussions and are likely to be the fixers or deal brokers (or, more likely, the delegates behind the power players in these roles). Get to know the *problem solvers* (though in all likelihood, they will reach out to you!).

Spoilers are difficult actors in a negotiation, requiring a large degree of finesse and interpersonal management. Although it is important to recognize these actors and their potential impact on a negotiation, their handling is usually best left to those with whom they have close relationships or whose authority they respect (including the Chairperson – see Chapter 6). *Spoilers* come in a variety of forms, but their defining characteristic is that they are determined to block an agreement – one way or another – if they don't get their way. When it comes to the final business of intervening to tank an agreement, spoilers are usually not subtle (read: drama will ensue); before that point, it may not be obvious what they are doing and they may not have even shown up for previous meetings. Among other motives, sometimes a spoiler believes this is the only way to do business; at other times, a spoiler becomes enthralled with the drama of conflict or her own ego, and occasionally, the spoiler loses a sense of reality amidst the alternate reality of a negotiation. The good news is that a strong Chairperson and insightful negotiators can mitigate the impact of a *spoiler*. Also, if you are on good terms with her, the *spoiler's* chances of directly harming you (while in the throes of her machinations) are reduced (though not eliminated).

Quiets and neutrals

Unlike the key personalities, the *quiets* and *neutrals* do not dominate conversations in a negotiating forum; in fact, you may not even hear, or notice, them at all. The *quiets* can often be found in the back rows of meetings (or entirely absent). They tend to avoid getting involved in the thick of debate and to steer clear of horse trading. Even on issues of interest to them, they seem to follow others, either preferring to have other delegates argue for them or carry them along. This "taking a backseat" is not necessarily a capacity issue, as delegates from smaller delegations can be very active. Instead, it may be because of personality preferences, because a delegate lacks instructions, or because the delegation's main priorities lie elsewhere. On the other hand, *neutrals*, by nature or instruction, prefer not to rock the boat. They are quite content to monitor the conversation from afar, jumping in only when absolutely necessary. Again, *neutrals* are such because of personality, instruction to be so, or because their delegation's priorities lie elsewhere as well.

It is easy to write-off *quiets* and *neutrals* because they may not speak up, regardless of appeals for help and despite extensive lobbying. Nevertheless, the two categories together usually make up the silent majority in a multilateral forum, and when they do move, you can expect big changes – or a big upset. They can also make or break the legitimacy of an outcome, even if they choose not to participate actively in the negotiation. The most successful negotiators attempt to build relationships with everyone, including the *quiets* and *neutrals*, because this can lead to wider acceptance of your positions. More importantly, you never know when you might need an ally, or just one more delegate to tip the balance in your favor.

Alliances

As we noted above, a negotiator's proposal (or even a neat solution to a dilemma) may meet resistance – or be all-out blocked – because of the negotiator herself or because she belongs to the "wrong" delegation. Above, we discussed personal rapport; here, we will deal with the delegation issue and how alliances can help.

The concept of the "wrong" delegation is a spillover effect from negotiators not being able to distinguish between the flag (or delegation), the individual, and the issue (including a good idea or a fair compromise). An example of this is the United States introducing any new idea – probably because some see the United States as a large, powerful country, with the ability to get its way. In general, some developing countries view ideas from developed countries with suspicion, and vice-versa. For example, if the P3 (France, UK, United States) were to propose a Security Council debate on "peace and security and development," it would likely be met with opposition by some developing countries; however, when Brazil proposed this controversial topic in 2011, there was no opposition and the debate was well attended. Likewise, when Bolivia proposed a draft resolution declaring an International Year of Quinoa in 2011, many developed countries objected due to suspicion over Bolivia's end goal. Some of these countries argued on the basis of there being a proliferation of international years on pet issues, even though they had regularly supported international years on other pet themes, either proposed by different sponsors or celebrating more "traditional" themes.

To overcome such programmed prejudice when tabling a proposal, a proponent has several options in the form of alliances (none of which are mutually exclusive):

- The first is to introduce the idea as a group proposal through a formal alliance, be it from an existing group or a new alliance forged to promote that particular initiative. With a number of delegations on board, it is possible to dilute the negative reaction to any particular proponent. For example, the G77 and China, as a group, tables several UN General Assembly resolutions each year, which is helpful because from among 134 Member States, it is often unclear which particular delegation is behind which idea in these resolutions.
- The second is to have a more "accepted" delegation present (or front) the proposal via a temporary alliance. For example, if an EU country wants to pursue an initiative on development, it might benefit from asking a supportive developing country to present the idea as its own, making it a developing rather than developed world proposal. The opposite scenario might work as well for a developing country's initiative on aid effectiveness. Such temporary (and potentially behind-the-scenes) alliances between developed and developing countries could give certain proposals a much higher chance of survival.
- The third option is to lobby respected negotiators from other delegations who will speak up for the proposal, thereby forming a flexible alliance:

Friendlies: Although *friendlies* can be useful here, their verbal support will have minimal impact because it is expected; they are more useful for adding to the numbers (to give the impression of a strong base of support) and to help bring others on board. They can also play the critical role of stand-ins – for example, Canada might introduce a U.S. proposal as its own, and thereby win it broader support.
Neutrals: The verbal support of a neutral delegation is more meaningful, as that delegation is not viewed as being automatically aligned with you. If you are an absolute poison pill, you need a neutral delegation, not just to speak up, but to introduce your idea for you.
Opponents: The support of a perceived opponent is the most powerful yet. If an opponent can support your proposal, that implies it has real merit and is worth considering. It is unlikely that an opponent would agree to serve as a proxy.

Forming alliances – be they formal, temporary, or problem-specific – is again where relationships come into play, because you are asking for explicit collaboration towards a common goal. Possibly, you are also asking someone to do something for you as you attempt to meet your delegation's goals. You cannot expect to do this without building relationships and maintaining your network. To determine your precise approach, it is important that you also read the dynamics in the room and understand the timeline and background of the negotiation (recall Chapter 3).

Networking

Now that we have established the importance of making friends and cultivating allies to achieve negotiation goals, this section will detail how we can better build these relationships. The most effective negotiators are well liked and respected because they undertake to be concertedly diplomatic, fair, and respectful of others. Even an *opposite* looking to prevent agreement due to national interests can mitigate the fall-out and subsequent blame on his country by being well liked and behaving considerately. If you practice the attributes of humility, fairness, and respect consistently, other delegates will try to help you, even if they don't share your position. But this requires you to network so that other negotiators can get to know you and your positive attributes and how you will contribute to a negotiation!

Build a networking plan for each negotiation, based on the positions you need to promote or defend. Use your own attributes to their best advantage, approaching networking as an integral part of your job.

Cheat Sheet for ~~Shooting in Archery~~ *Networking at the UN*

Step One: Survey the target board – *Look at key personalities chart* (see Chapter 3)

Step Two: Decide on your exact target – *If you are feeling like (a) a fish out of water, target one of the friendlies as part of your warmup; (b) the clock is ticking, target a key player; or (c) charming George Clooney, go get 'em tiger!*
Step Three: Check for external factors like weather and distractions – *Does your target look stressed, or about to rush off for a meeting? Recalibrate if so*
Step Four: Assume position – *Go up and introduce yourself. Relax and smile (as your target will feed off your vibe)*
Step Five: Aim – *Ask your target about her interest in [fill in subject]; invite subject to discuss further over coffee, where you can key off her expressed interested, thereby holding her attention*
Step Six: Release the string – *Let target respond*
Step Seven: Follow through – *If target is not available to talk at length now, ask for their contact info and email them to set up a follow-up session*

Some additional advice from our mothers: don't lie, be yourself, and don't do anything mom wouldn't do! One of us once made an (intimidating) opponent into a friend by explaining herself in the opponent's native tongue. This paid off literally years later in another venue on an entirely separate issue. As we said earlier, always build relationships – you never know when they will pay off!

Be wary, however, of getting too cozy with other negotiators. If you are always carrying the water for another delegation, no one will know whether the ideas are coming from you or them, and you can be viewed as a stooge. This can backfire both in the negotiation itself and with your handlers back in capital if they think you went soft and caved to a friend or did someone else's work.

Moving from venue to venue

Networking can be especially challenging for negotiators who move from venue to venue, as opposed to negotiators who are resident at a multilateral Mission, since there may be less time and fewer opportunities to build relationships. Some nomadic negotiators may go to several meetings for multiple UN agencies in the course of just a few weeks; others may attend one or two meetings a year. Non-resident delegates can also cycle out of assignments unexpectedly. As one example, negotiators in the UN climate change circuit tend to meet for a few days every few months. Even if you make headway with a delegate at one session, there is a chance she may not attend the next round, making it a little harder to "pick back up" the rapport the next time you both meet. In such cases, dropping her a note via email or WhatsApp to touch base can help keep the relationship warm in the interim. On the positive side, many nomadic negotiators end up on – or return to – the circuit for multiple years, making it possible to build strong and enduring relationships. Resident or itinerant, the time invested in networking is worth it.

Groups

Groups are a powerful, and in some cases permanent, form of alliance. They can augment a member delegation's influence and authority exponentially; they can also induce additional headaches, for both group members and those negotiating with them.

Big groups

The most powerful players in UN negotiations are often the representatives negotiating on behalf of the EU and G77. These individuals represent – and negotiate on behalf of – large groups of countries that have agreed to put forward a common position. The position that they are arguing in any given negotiation is already the result of hours of internal group negotiations, and often signifies an uneasy compromise. This makes group positions stronger, but also much less flexible. Particularly if a group works on the basis of consensus, its agreed position is likely to fall to the lowest common denominator.

Jamaican diplomat Nicholette Williams, who represented the G77 and China in negotiations on a sustainable development resolution told us:

> Although the text was presented by the G77 and China, arriving at a consensus in the Group was by no means an easy task. As the G77 consists of a broad cross-section of developing countries at varying levels of development, with divergent views, interests and concerns, the Group's deliberations on the various tenets of the resolution were long and quite painstaking.

Group dynamics

Groups are particularly attractive to small delegations. Apart from the readily available network for developing relationships and building alliances, these groupings are also useful sources of information and for sharing the negotiating workload. Small delegations often face a capacity challenge: there is too much work and there are too many issues to adequately address alone. Further, many delegations may not receive helpful instructions from capitals. Consulting with the group allows delegates to make sense of the load and promote a position helpful (in their view) to their country's goals. Even for delegations that group more due to like-mindedness than coverage needs, the burden sharing is helpful.

Ultimately, a group means you don't have to go at it alone. There is a power that comes from the numbers (especially when it is 134 versus 1!).

However, the internal dynamics of large groups also create problems. There are the endless negotiations before the actual negotiation to arrive at a group position – this takes time (hours, days, weeks) and effort (homework, late nights, arguing). It is tiring, especially when it all has to be repeated at the main negotiation later, and it can drain the limited pot of goodwill among some delegates before it is necessary. At UN Framework Convention on Climate Change meetings, for example, small island states meet for AOSIS coordination at 8am, then G77 coordination at 9am before formal meetings at 10am. After the formal negotiation meetings end in the evening, it is back to coordination meetings for even more group negotiations until late in the night.

One EU delegate shared that it often takes a lot of effort to strike the delicate balance needed in order to forge a common position among EU members. As such, when the EU subsequently negotiates with others, it can be difficult even trying to convince EU delegates to change the placement of a comma. This is because the internal EU agreement was so arduous to achieve that they fear any change, no matter how minor, might reopen the internal package deal.

During the main negotiation, other delegations within the group carefully watch (and sometimes second guess) the chosen spokesperson to be certain she is speaking for the group and pursuing the best outcomes. The choice of who is to be the group's spokesperson varies, e.g. it could be the country currently holding the EU presidency, it could be a delegate with known expertise who has the trust of the group, or it could be an unknown saddled with a job no one wanted. Members of groups don't always trust each other, though they need to appear to outwardly, and it is difficult for some negotiators to cede control to the group representative in the actual negotiation. Melding into a group is easier said than done for some. And some of the mistrust may be warranted: if the spokesman for the group doesn't have the right relationships, or poor judgment, that can ruin the outcome for the entire alliance.

Another concern about groups for those delegations within them, is that some may eventually cease to provide the needed safety in numbers that their members seek. Additionally, countries may feel constrained by their group because, while the members are fully aligned on one issue, they may have diverse positions on another. As political and economic alliances change, so – potentially – do the groupings that emerge and wane at the UN.

Other groups

Other useful groups may be permanent or semi-permanent, either region-, topic- or venue-specific, created with a view to promoting positions of mutual interest. For example, in climate change forums, there are several groups specific to that venue: the Umbrella Group, a loose coalition of non-EU developed countries, and the Environmental Integrity Group (EIG), a coalition comprising

Mexico, Liechtenstein, Monaco, the Republic of Korea and Switzerland. Examples of groups connected by common interests on development issues are: the Small Island Developing States (SIDS), Landlocked Developing Countries (LLDCs) and the Least Developed Countries (LDC). The Arab Group, composed of a number of Arab states, is an active block in some venues, as is the BASIC group of Brazil, South Africa, China, and India. Separately, there are formal UN regional groups that also serve as the basis for regionally-rotated UN positions. These are the African Group, Asia Pacific Group, Eastern European Group, Latin American and Caribbean Group (GRULAC), and the Western Europe and Others Group (WEOG).

There are quite a few "Friends of [include any subject here]" groups at the UN. These groups are created to galvanise support for a specific subject. As such, they are often cross-regional to boost their selling strategy (see Chapter 5 for more on selling strategy). This enables (a) wider outreach to countries when socialising the UN membership of the Friends' ideas, (b) more cooks invested in selling whatever comes out of the kitchen, and (c) more traction, since ideas from a Friends group are acceptable to a variety of countries across geographies and development status. Some Friends groups are short-term, e.g. Friends of Rio+20, which comprised some Second Committee delegates and was focused on getting discussions going on process and substance before the start of Rio +20 negotiations; others are longer term, e.g. Friends of Mediation, which supports and develops the use of mediation and meets even at the Ministerial level. Due to their cross-regional nature, Friends groups are important sounding boards and platforms for developing ideas that are likely to be acceptable to the wider UN membership.

Negotiating with groups

For non-groups, negotiating with a group can be downright annoying because a group negotiator has less flexibility than the negotiator for an individual delegation. "I can't agree, I have to consult with my group," becomes a common refrain – and it is both a tactic and a reality. This constraint applies not only to the individual group negotiator, but can impact the space for creative problem solving as well.

About the negotiations that developed the Sustainable Development Goals, former U.S. Ambassador to the UN's Economic and Social Council, Elizabeth Cousens commented that the novel structure of groups in that negotiation allowed significant space for more pragmatic thinking on a very complex issue. She told us,

> By negotiating individually or in unorthodox constituency groups, countries had a more direct way to table their interests and views. You might think that would make the negotiation more complex by adding more voices; in fact, it made solutions far easier by enriching mutual

understanding and "flooding the zone" with more opportunities for common ground.

Although groups can strengthen a country's voice, they may also diminish it.

Despite the headaches and the difficulties, and although alliances may change, the UN is unlikely to shy away from groups entirely in the long term. Given the amount of work, the power dynamics, and the state of the world, for many delegations, there is sometimes no alternative.

Conclusion

The old adage "you catch more flies with honey" aptly applies to the UN. In both networking and arguing a position, a negotiator can achieve her goals and gain allies with less effort (and even some benefits) by playing nicely with others. (Again, some intractable opponents are the exception to this, and then you may need to call in the theatrics (see Chapter 5).) Relationships are key for success. The true testament to the success of your relationships, however, is often clear only after you leave the negotiating forum. We are fortunate that many in our network have become true friends over time.

5 Welcome to negotiations theater: an off-Broadway production

In improv theater, a small portion of the performance may be pre-planned, while large parts are unscripted. The actors are on stage performing both the planned and impromptu elements, and will receive the public's accolades for a successful and entertaining show. The success of the production, however, really depends on the behind-the-scenes work of the backstage, sound, and light crews to keep up with – and even stay ahead of – the actors. There are also on-stage (official negotiations) and behind-the-scenes (unofficial negotiations) components in a UN negotiation. UN negotiations are like an improv act in that portions of the official meetings may be scripted, while others are impromptu, and the negotiators may be putting on a show, for each other, their countries, and/or other stakeholders.

This chapter shows how negotiators can better utilize the negotiation system once they understand it. By taking you behind the scenes of UN negotiations, we explain how and why agreements are forged and brokered outside of "formal processes." The chapter details why informal negotiations are important in negotiation processes and how they can be conducted. It also describes the essential elements of a formal UN meeting and offers insight into the pageantry at work. We also discuss the utility of what is often thought of at the UN as "negotiation theater."

Negotiating behind the scenes

Although there is often a large audience to attest to the progress of an official negotiation – the back-and-forth statements, the innumerable interventions, the proposals and counter proposals, and the presentation of a final compromise – much of the work that goes into constructing a successful negotiated outcome actually happens behind the scenes or in small group conversations outside the negotiation room. This is because less official arrangements can foster frankness and encourage creative thinking. In any negotiation, it is important to establish and organize the time and space for delegates to come together as individuals working toward a shared result.

To address difficult conversations

Every difficult conversation is about one or more of these three categories – facts, face, and feelings.[1] As Douglas Stone, Bruce Patton and Sheila Heen explain, the facts conversation is about what happened, what should happen, who is right and who is to blame. The face conversation is about how this difficult conversation affects our identity and what the issue means to us. The feelings conversation is often present but our inability to acknowledge and discuss these feelings openly usually complicates the difficult conversation.

Negotiations are filled with difficult conversations. It is, however, hard to address issues of facts, face, and feelings when there is a large audience. Venues need to be created so parties can have these difficult conversations outside of the public eye, including using the "ladder of inference" (explained in Chapter 2). Informal negotiations are this non-public venue.

Take for example, the negotiation on a Ten Year Framework of Programmes on Sustainable Consumption and Production (basically a work plan to address sustainable production and consumption – SCP for short) in 2011. The G77 and China, the EU, and the United States held very different views on key issues, including the establishment of a trust fund to finance the work and the list of actual programs (or work) that should be reflected in the final agreement. The United States was concerned about the cost, as well as avoiding implications for U.S. domestic law. Some countries from the G77 and China grouping were concerned that more developed countries might use the SCP framework as a tool to implement trade protectionist measures that would affect developing countries.

The lead negotiators from the G77 and China, the EU, and the United States met in the evenings, after formal negotiations had concluded for the day, to tackle some of these issues. They hoped to better understand each other's positions and to find common ground before they had to negotiate difficult sections of the proposed text in the formal negotiation process (in front of others). All G77 and China Member States were informed of these meetings and invited to participate – this transparency and inclusion was important to build trust. The G77 and China countries with key interests in the negotiations came to these evening meetings. Although they were quiet ("just there to listen") in the beginning, cautious of the motives of the United States and the EU, over the course of the week they became more comfortable within the small group setting and were willing to speak candidly about their concerns. Parties were now speaking to each other instead of at each other, which often happens on the "stage" of the formal negotiations. This allowed the United States to understand that others also had serious concerns about their domestic implications, and demonstrated to both the United States and the EU that the adoption of an SCP framework (a priority for both) was not a given. The informal setting therefore helped to keep tensions low, since such an extreme lack of mutual understanding can lead to fireworks (anger) in more formal discussions. These evening dialogues were an important breakthrough, enabling all parties to build the SCP framework together.

To brainstorm options

What is said in official negotiations (e.g. statements made, responses to questions, requests for clarification) is formally attributable to the delegation that the speaker represents. Statements are often available in the formal minutes of the meeting, and may also be communicated in press releases issued after the meeting, informal meeting notes from other delegates, or through a broadcast of the meeting itself (this now happens increasingly on the internet). As we discussed further below, official negotiations are thus useful for parties to deliver messages to larger audiences. On the downside, negotiators tend to be more guarded about proposing out-of-the-box options to address the subject at hand in official negotiations, for fear of attribution of a hare-brained idea to their delegation (also, it is generally good practice to try out new ideas on a small audience first). Informal negotiations provide this safe space for negotiators to brainstorm options without being "tied" to them.

Former U.S. Ambassador to the UN Samantha Power writes,

> It is well known that it was (former Russian Ambassador to the UN) Vitaly Churkin who raised his hand six times to veto Syria-related resolutions, but it is less known that it was Vitaly who worked frantically (and in the end futilely) to try to secure enough changes to the drafts that Moscow might support them.[2]

Negotiators need informal negotiation processes to explore and propose options that will not automatically be treated as their delegation's official position. For this reason, a large part of each UN resolution is hammered out in informal processes, e.g. over coffee between two delegations, on the sidelines of a formal meeting, or in an informal meeting of select delegates hosted by the Chairperson (or Chair).

To put together the final deal

> Thanks to the solidity and intensity of the long-lasting relationship between the small island developing states (SIDS) and the EU, and of the mutual respect and understanding of all participants of the negotiating process, all rounds of the informal consultations were held in a very constructive and friendly atmosphere. Of course, many informal-informals were held at the Delegates' Lounge in order to speed up the process of reaching agreement on the most difficult issues.
>
> As told to us by Jamaican diplomat Nicholette Williams and Polish diplomat Agnieszka Karpińska on representing the G77 and China and the EU respectively in negotiations on "Follow-up to and implementation of the Mauritius Strategy for the Further Implementation of the Programme of Action for the Sustainable Development of SIDS" during the 63rd session of the UN General Assembly.

In negotiations that involve multiple parties, the key players may come together informally to make difficult and complex tradeoffs aimed at cutting the final deal. Fewer players at the table translates into fewer conflicting interests (and reduces the noise in any compromise). The key negotiators can now focus on fitting their own interests into the final package. Such exclusive processes bet on the other players ultimately joining in their consensus (or, at least, a large part of it), or being too weak to hold the negotiations hostage until their objections are addressed.

Once an outcome is achieved within a small group, it is important to socialize it to the larger negotiating group before introducing it into the formal process. No one likes to be surprised, and the more delegations invested in – or at least convinced of – the outcome, the better. When socializing a proposal one should have a "selling strategy." This involves reaching out to key players (useful to refer to your key personalities chart first) and having a (or several) convincing narrative(s). When conducting outreach, remember to tailor the narrative to the stakeholder. A selling strategy may thus comprise different narratives, depending on the range of stakeholders one is reaching out to. However, the narratives should be genuine and not contradict each other as that can affect your credibility as an interlocutor.

Also, beware of buying too much into your own narrative. Much as in advertising, it is important to separate your pitch from your bottom line. For example, a marketing executive for a chocolate company may sell the merits of finishing each meal with chocolate, without necessarily following suit herself (for health reasons). When negotiators are unable to differentiate between the narrative employed by their country and their country's actual interests, they may take actions that inadvertently harm those interests.

An example of a small group process is the negotiations on the Copenhagen Accord by a small group of countries (including the United States, Brazil, India, China, and South Africa) on the sidelines of the 15th Conference of Parties of the UN Framework Convention on Climate Change. Although the group sought to provide the basis for a consensus that would subsequently be brought to the wider membership, many developing countries expressed concerns about the Accord and the Conference agreed only to "take note" of – rather than formally adopt – the "agreement."

If done well, small groups have the ability to develop the outcome – or at least the key compromises to get there – and it can subsequently be difficult to disrupt the small group's consensus that the chosen players have bought into. If the stakes in a negotiation are important to your delegation, you (the negotiator) need to be in the kitchen while the cooks are concocting the final deal. If not, it will be difficult to add your ingredients – or even spoil the pudding – later on. At the same time, the inability of this small influential group to achieve adoption of the Accord by the Conference (rather than just "taking note"), shows that small groups should take seriously the need for a broad and concerted selling strategy, so as not to get blindsided by uncertain support.

One psychological factor to remember is that those invested in an outcome are more likely to advocate for it; they are also more effective in doing so. It is therefore helpful, despite the additional mess, to invite more cooks into the kitchen. People like to be a part of the solution. And it always helps to have more people gunning for the solution – whatever it is – if you want it to succeed. Those invested will help to socialize, or "sell," the outcome as well. Involving key stakeholders in informal negotiation processes can result in greater investment in the success of the agreement reached in the informal process; the reverse is also true. Delegations can and will block an agreement, not because they disagree with the substance, but because they were not included in the consultation process.

Negotiating with capital

A negotiator's work is never done: once she has concocted the back-room deal with her colleagues, she has to sell that outcome to her delegation and capital before she can take part in its choreographed presentation. In a multilateral negotiation, a delegate representing her country is not only negotiating with the other delegates, but also with her handlers – or desk – back in her capital (and sometimes also with her group or delegation). Typically, because they have observed the entire process or they understand the local dynamics, the group and delegation on the ground are the easiest to convince of a legitimate compromise or a valid deal (though they aren't pushovers either). Capital, however, is another story. Removed from the context of the negotiation, the desk and the broader national interagency process it represents often does not understand the constraints under which a negotiator is operating.

At the beginning of a negotiation, a delegate optimally receives instructions - or guidance - in the form of clear parameters that provide a framework within which she can agree to variations on a country's goals. The guidance can be broad and thematic, or line-by-line based on the draft text. Regardless, a delegate's priorities should be clearly stated, in order of preference, and any redlines clearly delineated. Additionally, it is helpful for the negotiator to have an indication of which changes to the text are more "must-haves" and which are "nice-ifs." The best guidance also includes brief notes on precedent and related discussions in other fora, as well as a marking of how the text has changed from any previously agreed language (see Chapter 3). Optimally, guidance should be written in such a way that the delegate does not need to communicate back to capital at every stage of the negotiation, barring an entirely unforeseen development. It helps if the officers drafting the instructions have taken part in or observed multilateral negotiations, as it can be difficult to understand the context unless you have seen it in action. Guidance in hand, after reading the room, a delegate should be able to see her way to the fair outcome.

In the real world, guidance is rarely perfect and often incomplete – it is impossible, even for an experienced desk, to predict all the permutations; negotiators do not have perfect judgment, even within well-crafted guidelines; and the context and personalities in the room during any given negotiation can throw a wrench into even the most foolproof instructions. In short: life, and negotiations, are unpredictable. So when a negotiator is perceived to have deviated from her guidance – or not gotten exactly every priority in order – she may have some explaining, a little justifying, and a lot of convincing, to do in order for her capital to agree to an outcome. A good negotiator takes this into account, cultivating a strong relationship with her desk and communicating effectively with her capital about the context and dynamics throughout a negotiation. The more the desk trusts the negotiator, and understands her perspective, the stronger an ally it will be – a potentially necessary ally in her country's approval process. A strong relationship with her desk is also likely to get a negotiator better guidance in the future. A negotiator needs all the friends and allies she can get!

Communications with capital

Having been both desk and delegate at various points in our careers, we have learned that it improves the delegate/desk relationship and lays the groundwork for better guidance if a negotiator helps minimize the burden on an often overworked desk. A negotiator can mark up the first draft of a resolution under discussion, noting any deviations from expected language (or agreed language), and sharing any relevant political context, before sending it to capital for comment. She can also send regular (not real time) updates on the state of negotiations, noting where the guidance still holds and where additional input may be needed later. Describing the lay of the land and preparing the desk for the likely outcome well in advance will go a long way to build trust and demonstrate her efforts to meet the expected goals.

Negotiating at the table

Although much of the work essential to a good compromise takes place behind the scenes, the dynamics at the negotiation table have the potential to make or break a carefully crafted outcome. As we noted above, what a delegate says at the official negotiation table is formally attributable to the delegation she represents. Her words are often widely available on the internet to anyone interested in reading them (and Twitter has only added to the dissemination options). She therefore cannot say just anything, and – if she is appropriately strategic – every word she utters serves a specific purpose or sends a targeted message.

In the chair and at the microphone

All Member States of a UN entity have a seat and a right to speak at the formal negotiation table. Depending on the venue, certain observers and stakeholders have seats and speaking rights as well. The formal meetings are the platform from which participants in a UN meeting jointly send their agreed message to the world. Formal meetings and negotiations are also platforms for individual Member States to send messages to their various audiences. These include their stakeholders – those in the room, many of which have an agenda or are hoping for a specific result on at least one element of the outcome document – and at home. For example, the 1972 UN Conference on Environment and Development introduced the participation of Major Groups, representing sectors of society that had a role and interest in sustainable development; these representatives, along with various non-governmental organisations, often observe in formal and informal negotiations during relevant meetings. Occasionally, a delegation's statement has more to do with domestic politics than the international conversation at hand. For the most part, however, Member States are sending messages and signals to each other, staking out positions or conceding points in the negotiation at hand.

After the formalities of an official multilateral meeting, most negotiations take place around a table. Occasionally, delegates are facing the Chairperson, speaking to each other through microphones (sometimes with translation). There is almost always an audience – in addition to your fellow negotiators, there will be stakeholders, the Secretariat, various reporting services, and other staff from delegations (potentially including your boss).

In general, a delegate may speak when the Chair calls on her, called "taking the floor." Only one person from a delegation may speak at a time. A delegate typically attracts the attention of the Chair by "raising her flag" – either placing the delegation's placard sideways, if there is one, or briefly raising a hand. A word to the wise: don't raise your hand, as you did in school, but lift it to eye level in a visible gesture, ensuring you catch the Chair's eye. It is sometimes difficult for the Chair to discern the order of a raised placard or hand – so be patient with the Chair, but don't let yourself be overlooked.

Formals vs. informals

The formal component of a meeting – usually called the Plenary – almost always involves a microphone. Each delegation has a placard at its seat and in most cases, the chairs face forward, such that delegates face the Chairperson rather than each other. It usually takes place in a large room in front of an expansive audience, including non-negotiators. This is usually the starting scene of each negotiation process, after which the actual negotiations proceed, either formal negotiations in Plenary or informal negotiations (still quite formal, in many cases), in the same room or elsewhere. The differences between formal and informal negotiations – in format and formality – will depend on the venue. Historically, the Chair would read through a draft outcome paragraph by paragraph, calling on delegates in order, who took turns intervening on items of interest and requesting additions, deletions, or edits; increasingly, Chairs now ask for comments on sections of a document before delving into the paragraph-by-paragraph details.

One example of an informal negotiation process practiced within the Committees of the UN General Assembly is "informal informals." In these meetings, there are no microphones or placards, the room is small, and – a game changer from negotiations in Plenary – delegates face each other around a table. Although negotiators are still performing for an audience, it is much smaller, and the altered seating arrangements greatly improve communication.

Speaking

A brief note on statements and interventions – a statement is a delegation's formal message on an item, be it substance or process, while an intervention is literally an interruption. Most negotiations take place via interventions. Although both are technically formal, a statement is more so; it is also more likely to be recorded in the official record. Either can feature in notes, news reports or (increasingly) tweets.

Negotiation theater

When difficult conversations need to happen in the public space of formal, informal, or informal informal negotiations, theater can ensue. For an experienced negotiator, the use of theater is a strategic move, calculated to get to the best outcome, usually when there is an intractable delegate or irreconcilable issue. Delegates also employ theater to act out a final compromise in the public space; the use of theater in this case helps demonstrate to the "audience" the legitimacy of an outcome negotiated behind the scenes. There are different manifestations of negotiation theater, some constructive and some destructive. We discuss the most common below.

Posturing

Posturing is just what it sounds like; it is when a delegate blusters, bluffs, or threatens in order to get a result. In some circumstances, posturing is justifiable; in others, it is essentially bullying, which is at best the hallmark of insecurity and at worst inexcusable. Justifiable posturing can be employed when a delegate has instructions to convey a message or adopt a posture that is not conducive to compromise (it sounds odd, but trust us, it happens). It is also useful in defending an unpopular position that has no support. In such a cases, the delegate may need to posture in formal statements and informal interventions, while working constructively on the sidelines to ensure an acceptable outcome. The purpose of the posturing is to send the necessary public message – either to other Member States, certain stakeholders, or a domestic audience; though not optimal, it is sometimes obligatory.

The other side of posturing is that exhibited by the blusterer or spoiler who threatens extreme consequences – global, national, personal – if she doesn't win on a certain point or get her way on a specific issue. In this case, posturing is used to bully other delegates. Although posturing may allow the delegate a complete coup in one negotiation (in terms of winning all the points possible for her delegation), she will lose overall, as such behavior destroys her credibility. Other delegates will also begin to understand they are dealing with a blusterer and ignore her empty threats in future.

Acting

Drama – essentially faking emotion – can be used in certain circumstances to break through an impasse or get through to an irretrievably intractable delegate. It can be useful in getting to a fair outcome with difficult negotiators (see example in Chapter 4) or when the group negotiating has gotten lost in the negotiation itself, because sometimes an emotional outburst can have the impact of jarring delegates out of a rut or negotiation-induced alternate reality. The negative form of acting is when a negotiator uses tantrums or insincere entreaties, unnecessarily, to get her way. It is best to minimize drama and heightened emotions (which lead to misunderstandings) in a negotiation, so theatrics should be used judiciously.

An experienced negotiator sometimes employs a form of acting that is more akin to exaggeration. She may exaggerate the degree of an issue or concern in order to underline a point, ensure a priority is respected, or emphasize the importance of a concession, all to help her position. Finally, any acting – be it theatrics or exaggeration – should really be acting. Your real emotions should be kept in check, as they can impact your ability to see outcomes clearly; remember, it is not personal, and emotions in negotiations can be a liability.

Denouement: acting out the compromise

The final – and most valuable – form of theater is the choreographed exchange acted out to introduce a final compromise in a formal negotiation. It is basically the dramatic reenactment – much compressed – of the behind-the-scenes compromise process. Such choreography helps legitimize the outcome forged behind the scenes and demonstrates to those watching how the delegations have evolved towards the compromise.

At times, the situation may call for "The Merchant of Venice," where a negotiator agrees to compromise on issue A after appearing to extract a pound of flesh from her counterpart by having the latter compromise on issue B. Another approach is the "Romeo and Juliet," where negotiators publicly appear to "kill" (i.e. drop from consideration) issue C; meanwhile, they have agreed behind the scenes that they will resurrect issue C in a different forum in order to avoid the issue in the current negotiation. Then there is "The Taming of the Shrew," where negotiators appear to bring an unwilling party into the fold through the formal negotiation process, when this was – in reality – worked out behind the scenes before the formal meeting. Sometimes these reactions or responses help to legitimize the outcome in the eyes of the audience. In other cases, delegates must react to preserve a national position or send a message home. Regardless, they help bring closure to the negotiation. In accepting a role in this production, it is important to determine the impact of your words – read the dynamics in the room to be sure your acting doesn't undermine the outcome you have worked so hard to achieve.

A word of advice

Posturing, acting, theatrics, staging, and choreography are all realities at the UN. As we have discussed, these can be positively or negatively employed, but they are present and prevalent. It is therefore important to know how to use and respond to such tactics appropriately. We believe that negotiations would be better without all the drama, if delegates were able to be genuine and earnest and just dive into "problem-solving with friends" (as we like to think of negotiations). Unfortunately, entrenched interests, insecurities, egos – and sometimes instructions – just don't allow this. Occasionally, a fair outcome demands artifice. While we do acknowledge this and recognize their utility, we don't promote such tactics. We would urge negotiators – and delegations – to move beyond the theatrics to the extent possible – to protect their positions *and* work together for the greater good.

Building consensus through formal and informal processes at the UN - the SCP Story

Returning to the example of the SCP negotiation in 2011, the lead G77 and China negotiators were unsure if UN Member States would agree to their idea to delete the entire preamble of the Chair's negotiating text. To push this proposal, they convened a G77 and China SCP core group. While all G77 and China countries were invited to participate in this group, only those who were keenly interested in the issue turned up for meetings. This helped to narrow down who were the key players and stakeholders within the G77 and China for this negotiation.

The lead G77 and China negotiators then added their recommendations in the first draft of the Chair's negotiating text, including deleting the preambular section. This was circulated to the core group for discussion. Once they had the core group's buy-in, the text was discussed at a formal G77 and China meeting. As the lead negotiations had already engaged the interested parties in the G77 and China through the core group meetings, they were able to forge a G77 and China position on the Chair's negotiation text without much difficulty. They also primed the EU and the U.S. delegations on some the proposed amendments so that their counterparts would not be caught by surprise at the start of the formal negotiation process and take up a defense posture in response.

While this approach was against the norm, it made for a more effective negotiation process, enabling all UN Member States to focus their energies on getting the key sections of the SCP framework right. Other upsides to bringing to the G77 and China a negotiation text with recommendations supported by the core group were that it enabled a more organized discussion of the text with the larger G77 and China membership; and countries were less inclined to pepper the text with amendments that had little value, keeping the text clear and more concise.

Conclusion

Ultimately, official and informal negotiation processes feed off each other, and the latter is essential to the former. While informal negotiation processes are important for building understanding and often necessary for finding real compromises, official negotiations are indispensable for other purposes. Official negotiations allow delegations to go on the record with their positions and demonstrate their priorities. They also allow delegations that were not a part of informal processes to feel that they are a part of the overall process, allowing them to have their say. It additionally allows delegations who were part of the compromise to state their core positions, explain their concessions, and assert reservations if needed. The formal negotiations are the stage for diplomatic theater: small countries can call out large countries here, and large countries can assert dominance or appear kindly – it is about each delegation creating a perception and sending a message. Sometimes this message is for other delegations, as a matter of foreign policy; sometimes it is for stakeholders or the international community; sometimes, it is for the delegation itself, or for the handlers back in capital, or even domestic politics for a domestic audience. It is often posturing, and sometimes saving face – occasionally it is ground-breaking goodwill. Finally, the formal negotiations, in a public venue with everyone present, give the outcome legitimacy.

Notes

1 Douglas Stone, Bruce Patton, and Sheila Heen, *Difficult Conversations: How to Discuss What Matters Most* (New York: Penguin, 2011), Kindle edition.

2 Samantha Power, "Samantha Power: My friend, the Russian Ambassador," *The New York Times*, 25 February 2017.

6 I call this meeting to order: Chairing UN negotiations

As the elected Chairperson (Chair, for short) enters the conference room, everyone knows who she is. When she sits in her chair, she is likely to find: a prepared script, a list of speakers (if Member States were asked to indicate ahead of the meeting), and a small object that looks like a hammer (which she will use to bring the room to order or to gavel the final negotiated agreement). Beside and behind her sit her support team. The stage is set and, if this meeting is open to the media, the cameras are on. The Chair has a clear view of all delegates and the Member States' nameplates shine in front of each familiar face. Depending on the procedures for the meeting, civil society representatives may also be there, circling the edges of the room, among the Secretariat and other stakeholders.

Over the years, the Chair has learned not to confuse a country's position with the individual representing it. She has found good friends from countries that hold views directly contrary to her own country's ideology. Like sifting through sand to find gold, one of her skills is to distinguish between posturing and real interests because what is said at the microphone in the plenary room is not necessarily what the delegation really seeks in the negotiation (as discussed in Chapters 2 and 5). At the beginning of the negotiation process, her credibility is still intact – she will work hard to keep it; this is her most precious resource, the one that will allow her to build trust among the group assembled before her and to nudge them towards a common outcome. Also important is her integrity, which will guide her through the difficult choices she may need to make in order to faithfully fulfill her duty to the delegates and the process.

Ideally, the Chair is similar to an orchestra conductor in that she is responsible for leading the ensemble and drawing the right sounds and silences from the delegates to make music, while garnering the necessary support from the wider audience and other stakeholders. At the UN, the Chair needs to understand the big picture, but not necessarily be an expert on the subjects being negotiated (although that helps!). Instead, she needs to be an expert on the process – every negotiation is a ritual. She needs to be familiar with the particular norms, spoken and unspoken, of this forum, before sitting in *that* chair.

Chairing is personal

Chairs are usually appointed in a personal capacity; i.e. a Chair is the individual, not the country. This concept of "personal capacity" is important to the legitimacy of a multilateral process. Ideally, a Chair tries to be neutral and without agenda. However, some Chairs have difficulty remembering this; additionally, some delegates misattribute national motivations and delegation priorities to the Chair's actions when that might not be the case. Although neutrality is the ideal rather than the reality, as we discuss below, it should always be the Chair's objective.

Exceptions to the "personal capacity" rule are conferences held outside of UN headquarters, in which case the Chair is often a high-level official from the host country. Nonetheless, the expectation remains that the Chair will put aside her national position – at least to some extent – in order to effectively facilitate the multilateral process and mediate among the various positions.

Chairing a multilateral process – particularly on topics of global relevance – can be a deeply personal experience, exhausting but also immensely rewarding. There is a certain camaraderie that develops among delegates working diligently together, composed of understandings – and friendships – that can last a lifetime. There is also the permanence (hopefully!) of the globally-significant outcome that you – the Chair – helped to bring into the world.

Attributes of a good Chair: process and conduct

As Ambassador Tommy Koh, who masterfully presided over the UN Conference on the Law of the Sea, the Earth Summit, and many other distinguished processes, has written in "The art of chairing conferences,"[1] a piece we include at the end of this chapter, a successful Chair exhibits specific behaviors and qualities, including being humble, respectful, fair, transparent, trustworthy, a good listener, proactive, calm, courageous, a good mediator and bridge builder, and inspiring, among others. Ambassador Koh also recommends nine approaches for a successful Chairpersonship: (i) master your brief; (ii) use your bureau; (iii) work with the secretariat; (iv) be a team player and team builder; (v) avoid setting up secret negotiating groups; (vi) create an inclusive, transparent and orderly negotiation process; (vii) respect the importance of timing; (viii) actively garner support and seek to accommodate; and (ix) work well with the NGOs.

These items can be encapsulated in two words: process and conduct. Effective Chairs understand, and use to their best advantage, the negotiation process, while conducting themselves in a manner that inspires confidence in the process and their Chairpersonship. While the list of approaches may seem long, the good news is that if you follow them, you can avoid the usual pitfalls! Also, many of them – the behaviors and qualities – can be learned, becoming second-nature with enough practice. Below we explain more about the Chair's role in the process itself. We also delve into some additional nuances to consider and traps to avoid.

Steering the process

Drafting proposals

The Chair usually holds the pen over the negotiated outcome. She gets to draft – and often redraft (with help from key delegates and the Secretariat) – the text that will attempt to balance the different interests of the parties to a negotiation. This task is essential to a successful negotiated outcome.

She typically begins her Chairpersonship by meeting with key delegations to get a sense of the dynamics as well as their initial buy-in for her proposed working methods. She then holds a few meetings with all the Member States to allow for exchange of views, such as on priority areas of work as well as the process. If the Member States are ready to make progress, they may call on her to put forward a negotiation text (sometimes known as the Chair's text) or a compilation text (a document that has all the unadulterated proposals of the Member States). These documents are usually prepared with the help of the UN Secretariat.

A wise Chair is also likely to consult key delegations on her Chair's text, including making amendments, – to secure their non-objection – before formally tabling the text to the wider membership. Here, it is worth noting that if a Chair's initial draft is too close to what the eventual outcome could look like, the spoilers may pull the text to one extreme during the negotiation process because they are not ready to compromise, versus the moderates who may be more welcoming of the draft. As a result, the negotiation gets skewed in one direction.

If the Chair feels the timing is right, she may put forward the Chair's text without a formal mandate from the negotiation process, on "the Chair's responsibility." If, however, she has misjudged, and delegations are not yet ready to see a Chair's draft, she can expect delegations to argue that "the Chair has no mandate" to draft an outcome, or that her proposal "has no status in the negotiations." There are also occasions where the Chair starts with an initial negotiating text tabled by the key proponent or group of proponents of an issue. Regardless, the Chair (with the help of the Secretariat) must edit the document – however it came into being – after several rounds of negotiations, taking into account the interests, including specific text amendments, of the negotiators.

In order to draft a compromise text or "Chair's proposal," on a paragraph, section, or the entirety of an outcome document, a Chair must listen to the stated positions, seek to understand the underlying interests, and creatively use language to solve perceived disagreements and resolve differences in position. Sometimes, she must give something to one delegation in one area, and take something from the same delegation in another. Overall, her drafting must appear to be fair to the negotiators at the table.

In drafting, the Chair may be working with a complex negotiated text that contains many different sections. These sections are like pieces in a puzzle; in the end, all the pieces need to come together into a cohesive whole. To make this happen, the Chair needs to make sure that each section fits with the rest of the text and that each piece is acceptable to all the parties. The idea of "nothing is agreed until everything is agreed" must be the Chair's mantra and guiding principle. The authors have witnessed several UN meetings during which an outcome was not agreed by Member States because there was language in only one section that was not acceptable to some delegations, even though the rest of the text was entirely acceptable to all. To avoid this scenario, the Chair needs to keep her eye on the entire puzzle as it is being put together.

Timing

The Chair also determines the pace at which the parties discuss and negotiate the text. The pace of a negotiation is, for example, how quickly the first and second readings of the draft document take place, when a new version of the text – based on negotiator interventions – is introduced, when a Chair's proposal is presented, and when a Chair holds informal meetings between key players. In this sense, the Chair controls the rhythm in a negotiation, just as the conductor keeps time in the orchestra. If the Chair's pace is too slow, missing cues that agreement is at hand, delegations can become exasperated; boredom offers excess time to cause trouble. If the Chair proceeds too quickly, forcing agreements or pushing proposals before it is time, she may not have the time and space to build the trust and goodwill she needs among the negotiators, and between the negotiators and herself, that is necessary to support her proposed solutions. Time and space are also needed for each negotiator to gain confidence in the Chair's leadership and in the process.

Reading the room – and the possibilities

The duties of the Chair are manifold, and they change during the course of the negotiation. At times, the Chair needs to be a mediator between parties; at others, an admonishing parent, and at other critical moments, an encouraging cheerleader, allowing the parties to resolve issues by themselves. Offering too many suggestions to break deadlocks can lead negotiating parties to rely too much on the Chair to resolve all the problems in the negotiation process.

For example, in a negotiation on a UN General Assembly resolution that one of us chaired, the Chair regularly proposed alternative language and other solutions whenever there were any differences in the Members' positions. As a result, the negotiators relied on the Chair for solutions and felt no pressure to find mutually agreeable solutions; the hardliners stayed particularly firm, with no incentive to budge from their positions. Some pressure is important in a negotiation process to catalyse the negotiators to solve their own disagreements when they can. It was only when the Chair realized her mistake, and made clear to the negotiators that the success or failure of this resolution was no longer in her hands, that the hardliners finally began proposing solutions to bridge the gaps.

On the other hand, some negotiators may protest if they view the Chair as controlling, rather than mediating, the dialogue. Chairing is a delicate balance. Ultimately, the power to determine and agree to the actual outcome and the particular language in the outcome lies in the hands of the negotiators and not the Chair, albeit the Chair does have considerable influence in shaping the outcome. The Chair will need to listen for the cues in negotiators' interventions to determine what the overall piece should sound like, what the outcome document should look like, and guide them towards it.

Overall, the Chair needs to steer the intergovernmental process forward, helping parties reach a sustainable outcome; this does not always mean a document adopted by consensus in the General Assembly. For example, there are situations in which parties are not ready to agree to a strong outcome and the Chair instead needs to pursue "low-hanging fruit," or be satisfied with no outcome at all. In such cases, she may need to refrain from proposing quick fixes that could hurt the possibility of forging a better outcome in the future. To do her job well, the Chair must be attuned to the interests of the delegations in front of her in order to set the right pace and expectations. Moreover, the Chair has to manage the emotional currents that are always present in a negotiation, such as fear, pride, and suspicion.

A good Chair – the Sustainable Development Goals (SDGs) story

The SDGs took about four years to negotiate. The process was complex, beginning with an open-ended working group (OWG) and then continuing in formal intergovernmental negotiations. In this two-phased approach, Macharia Kamau, the Ambassador of Kenya, co-chaired the entire process. Ambassador Csaba Körösi of Hungary co-chaired the OWG and Ireland's Ambassador David Donoghue co-chaired the intergovernmental process.

Setting the agenda

The co-chairs designed a strategic agenda, bringing experts in each field in to speak on the subject of every potential goal. These exchanges with scientists, economists, and other experts better informed the diplomats on the subject matter in advance of negotiations. The co-chairs also delayed the process of drafting the goals and targets, launching more than 12 months into the process! This allowed the negotiators a substantial period of building trust and knowledge on the issues.

Managing emotions

As the tension in the room rose, the co-chairs maintained their calm and used their senses of humor to manage the emotions in the room.

Keeping it inclusive

The co-chairs led a very inclusive process. In addition to holding mostly open meetings that included all delegations, they met with civil society representatives every morning during the negotiation sessions, allowing for other creative ideas to flow into the formal process. This also helped in building ownership of the outcome, with and beyond governments.

Holding the pen

Despite pressure from some delegations to negotiate the SDGs "word by word," the co-chairs kept the pen themselves, unveiling new versions of the text in response to each round of negotiations. This was important as it kept the text congruent. Sometimes, when delegations start drafting text word by word, no one outside the walls of the UN can understand what was agreed!

Package deals

The co-chairs were able to mediate between parties and several goals were final compromises that came as a "package deal." For example, many developing countries wanted SDG 17 on means of implementation but did not want SDG 16 on peaceful societies, whereas many developed countries wanted the opposite. The co-chairs were able to prepare a final draft that included both in acceptable forms, keeping a balance between the interests of all countries.

Process options

The UN is a hierarchical organization: all protocol is guided by rank. The higher the rank, the more privileges an individual has at a meeting. It is similar to the experience of being at an airport, where those traveling in business get to board the plane first. Speaking order at high-level meetings may therefore be: Presidents, Prime Ministers, Ministers, Ambassadors, and then the rest of us. However, protocol does not always dictate process, and a Chair needs to consider the timing and structure of both the formal and informal components of a negotiation, and how they fit together, in order to succeed.

In a formal process, everyone is invited – all delegations and accredited organizations are there, and the meeting is webcast. The formal component of a meeting also has an agenda with a list of items that everyone can see, and on which they will be able to voice opinions. To continue with the image of the airport: in a formal process, no matter whether you are sitting at the tail end of the plane or in the first row, you are still on board the same plane as everyone else, and you know the final destination.

Beyond the formal process, there is the informal process (or processes). These are unique to each negotiation, and sometimes need to be tailored to the individual delegates participating; there is no fixed practice. If there is enough trust in the room, the informal process can be rather simple; for example, the Chair may convene several small meetings with key delegations to discuss the main issues in the negotiated text. As we discussed in Chapter 5, delegates feel more at ease to explore possible options in smaller meetings (and make trade-offs more easily) than in large official Plenary meetings with eyes watching and machines recording.

However, if the issue is important and there is insufficient trust, then the informal process becomes a very delicate matter. Like fragile glass, the Chair needs to handle the dynamics with the utmost care in order not to shatter the possibilities. In such cases, a poor reaction from a delegation that feels "left out" of a smaller group meeting can jeopardize the entire negotiation.

For example, at certain points in the climate talks leading to the Paris Agreement (2009–2015) there was so little trust among delegations that the informal process required rigid structures. In fact, it often took days to even agree on the formal agenda, let alone any substance! Building trust in an intergovernmental negotiation is one of the most important jobs of the Chair. At every step, she needs to keep everyone informed and on board; no passenger can "feel" left out. In the absence of trust, delegations start to sabotage the process and the focus turns to the procedures rather than the substance.

Without trust, it is difficult to make music

The Presidency for the climate talks in 2010 (officially titled the 16th Conference of the Parties to the United Nations Framework Convention on Climate Change, or COP 16) is an example of a chairmanship that needed to build trust in a shattered intergovernmental process. The COP 16

Presidency received the climate change process in shambles: no outcome had been agreed in the previous session and the level of trust was very low among delegations.

To ameliorate this trust deficit, the Presidency devoted its time and resources to making everyone feel included in the climate talks. They met with all delegations on the sidelines, ensuring that everyone felt heard. Moreover, they gave potential spoilers leadership roles, such as facilitator positions, so they would be more cooperative and have a stake in achieving the outcome. The venue of the conference induced calm – it was by a beautiful beach, in an all-inclusive resort. Most importantly, the Presidency focused on achieving the "low-hanging fruit." They knew that the timing was not ripe to achieve ambitious outcomes, but they were able to steer the process in the right direction. Regaining some trust in the intergovernmental process was the most important result achieved that year, which paved the way for the Paris Agreement.

The Secretariat

The importance of the Secretariat in the UN's work probably deserves its own book. Here, we highlight a few key points on the Secretariat's role in UN negotiations.

As stated earlier, Chairs are not always experts on the subjects being negotiated. As such, they rely on the expertise of UN Secretariat staff who work on these issues day in and day out, and who know the histories and potential landmines. These are professionals – international civil servants – dedicated to carrying out the actions that Member States agree. When one of us chaired a UN General Assembly resolution, it was thanks to the expert advice and patience of the UN Environment Programme staff sitting beside her that she managed to bring the resolution to successful adoption.

And it is not only Chairs who rely on the Secretariat; negotiators also tap the Secretariat for its knowledge and expertise. For example, when one of us was first tasked to negotiate the 10 Year Framework of Programmes on Sustainable Consumption and Production on behalf of the G77 and China, she had no background on the work that had been done over the past few years leading up to that negotiation. Thankfully, the Secretariat helped to bring her up to speed and was always available whenever she had any questions.

The Secretariat is also often the implementer of many UN agreements. It is thus useful to check in with them to see whether the proposals being discussed in a negotiation are realistic and feasible. After all, it is not particularly helpful for a negotiated outcome to look good on paper, but not be implementable, unless, of course, that was actually the point of the negotiation (and it sometimes is to keep the peace!).

That said, there are also times when turf wars between the various UN agencies or units in the UN Secretariat can complicate a negotiation – every department or office wants its perceived share of the pie ("glory" and additional resources). This is disappointing. Member States also sometimes take the concept of a "Member State driven organization" too far when they mute the Secretariat, preventing it from proposing ideas and offering its perspective. In UN negotiations, the Secretariat often cannot speak unless it is called upon to do so by a Member State; Member States too often fail to call on Secretariat input. This can be a wasted opportunity, as negotiators certainly do not have a monopoly on solutions to the serious challenges that the world is facing.

Indeed, there is sometimes mistrust and misunderstanding between Member State representatives and the UN Secretariat. This is a disappointment given that both groups must rely on each other, and that the UN could not function without both. As Farrukh Khan, former negotiator for the G77 and China and a member of the UN Secretariat told us:

> *Having served on both sides of the aisle, it strikes me that Member States and the Secretariat often fundamentally misunderstand each other. The UN bureaucracy appears to disdain negotiators and the governments they are supposed to assist and represent; many consider Governments and their representatives as barriers to effective progress, which they sincerely believe they could achieve alone. On the other hand, the negotiators and their governments seem to think the UN bureaucracy has very little to offer intellectually, believing not only that they are inherently incapable of understanding the complexity of the circumstances, and the perspectives that negotiators and governments bring, but that most of the UN bureaucracy is biased towards one ideological approach or another. In sum, to both camps, we can ascribe mistrust and misunderstanding, which can lead to failure – and there have been many. But fortunately, at the UN, failures can eventually be pathways to progress and opportunities to learn from mistakes. The adoption of the SDGs and the Paris Agreement are remarkable examples of such competing and contradictory perspectives coming together. Remarkable agendas emerged from both and – more importantly – both were occasions when the UN bureaucracy and the governments and its negotiators found themselves on a single page. To make progress, governments and the Secretariat need to work together and respect each other.*

Types of Chairs

In our years negotiating in multilateral fora, we have encountered many types of Chairs. We have also been in that position ourselves. Although we describe three general types of Chairs here, there is no formula that will guarantee a successful Chairmanship. There are, however, certain mistakes that can be easily avoided by reflecting on the following general characterizations.

Neutral Chair

Although there is no such thing as an entirely neutral Chair, there are many examples of individuals who have been able to set aside their national position to some extent in order to act as credible facilitators shepherding the group to reach the best collective outcome, even when this outcome is not entirely aligned with their delegation's goals. If diplomats are like soldiers in that each comes to battle with specific instructions from capital, the Chair is temporarily situated in the middle of that battle. Her mission is not to advance her own country's position – she does not fight for any side – but rather to find solutions that will help all the soldiers to turn a little and move in a common direction. This is the optimal type of Chair, assuming they are able to maintain the trust of the group and have an understanding of how to properly control the pace and dynamics of the negotiation to find the right compromise. Neutral Chairs are hard to find, as negotiators may not be able (for many different reasons) to put aside their country's position to advance what is in the best interest of a global outcome.

A biased Chair

A Chair may try to take sides if she has either a national or a personal agenda; regardless, a Chair's pursuit of an agenda represents a conflict that impacts the outcome of a negotiation. If the Chair needs to defend her national position as well as facilitate overall agreement among the group, it means the Chair now has to act as a facilitator and as one of the other delegations voicing their interests in the room. In this case, the Chair can easily abuse her power in order to tilt the negotiations towards outcomes that meet her national priorities. Like a doctor being asked to perform surgery on a family member, the Chair needs to have sufficient emotional and psychological distance from the issue in order to see the various delegations' points of view and to help parties reach common ground. Another potential conflict – and one we strongly advise against – is when the Chair favors or takes sides due to a personal agenda, including personal preferences, such as friendships or biases. In such cases, a Chair has lost sight of her duty as the director of the orchestra; she has abdicated the responsibility she accepted in agreeing to facilitate the negotiation.

Chair as host

There are many instances when the Chair of a negotiation is also the host of a conference. This is a difficult position, as the pressure to achieve a successful outcome rests disproportionally on the shoulders of the Chair as host. Many multilateral outcomes carry the name of the place they were negotiated, such as the Paris Agreement on Climate Change, the Monterrey Consensus, or the Uruguay Round in the context of the World Trade Organisation. Although a host Chair may be neutral in terms of not having an explicit agenda on the substance of the outcome, she may not truly be neutral because of the importance her government places on achieving a successful outcome; often, the host country wants an "ambitious," news-worthy outcome. This is also a sort of agenda.

As host, the Chair controls additional resources to support a successful outcome, including the choice and arrangement of a venue for the conference, control of the flow of the agenda, and the option of hosting state dinners and other side events. The Chair should use these in support of the outcome and to move the negotiations forward. Negotiators who are in good spirits may be more likely to work together towards common agreement.

For example, in one UN negotiation, the co-chairs provided free breakfast, lunch and dinner to all the negotiators. Not only did this build goodwill for the co-chairs, the negotiators met each other at the buffet table before going to the negotiating table. This served to break the ice and helped created a more cordial negotiating atmosphere overall. In contrast, one multilateral negotiation was held in a city in the middle of winter, where food was scarce at night, the venue was cold and impersonal, and delegates suffered from lack of sleep (and sunlight) for several consecutive weeks; the negotiation ended in failure. While this failed outcome cannot entirely be pinned on the bleak atmosphere, the negative impact the atmospherics had on the negotiators certainly did not help matters.

A good example of an advantageous use of resources is the 2015 Paris Climate Change Conference (COP 21), where the hosts, in this case the French government, introduced a number of innovations that helped the negotiations move forward. First, they flipped the high-level event, where Heads of State participate, to take place at the beginning rather than the end of the Conference. This change significantly improved the momentum of the negotiations, as Heads of State committed to the Paris deal in advance of having an outcome, resulting in these leaders applying pressure on their delegates to finalize the agreement (especially regarding the level of ambition to which they had already agreed!). If this high level event had taken place at the end of the negotiation process, as is typical of such Conferences, the Heads of State would have modified their positions to align with the highs and lows of the previous two weeks of negotiations and would likely have been less ambitious. Another example was the French government's offer of two tickets for each delegation to participate in the informal round-tables. This ensured that all delegations would have seats at the table, and no delegation could argue that the informal process was not inclusive or transparent.

Potential pitfalls for an intrepid Chair

In addition to the types of Chairs, defined by the situation in which a Chair finds herself, the character of the Chair also comes into play in a negotiation. As we noted at the beginning of the chapter, credibility and integrity are paramount to a successful tenure as Chair. Below are three mistakes guaranteed to compromise these essential qualities.

Overzealous Chair

An overzealous Chair attempts – at all costs – to achieve an outcome agreed by consensus, even if the consensus is not there. This can happen when a Chair associates the success of the Conference or outcome with her own, or when she sees the outcome as a vanity project. She then exerts all her powers – good and bad – in order to succeed. In one meeting we attended, an overzealous Chair gaveled a document so quickly that delegates did not even have time to object before it was adopted; this led to questions being raised about the legitimacy of the outcome. A Chair is quite powerful in that the result of her Chairmanship lives on, regardless of how many support it. That said, a Chair does not really have unlimited power, especially because, if she behaves badly, she will not be asked to chair again. If a Chair is overzealous, she may push proposals through too early, or rush the process entirely, before the timing is ripe[2] for compromise.

Drunk with power

Another common ailment of the Chair is a well-known malady of the human condition: power can corrupt even the best character. From her place at the center of the negotiation process, the Chair can temporarily lose sight of her humble role as facilitator for her fellow delegates. She may seek to take over the process or unduly influence the outcome, out of a misguided sense of self-importance or vanity. A Chair that forgets her place is not yet ready for the role.

Chair as punching bag

When a process is not proceeding well, the easiest and most visible person often gets the blame, whether they deserve it or not. In a negotiation, this is often the Chair. In extreme cases, the Chair can even become the victim of a negotiation gone awry. At some moment in almost every negotiation, the Chair becomes the punching bag. Everyone can blame the Chair for an uncomfortable exchange between delegates, not offering enough time to reflect, giving delegations too much time to cause trouble, a poorly-timed compromise proposal, or the failure of the meeting.

Conclusion

Before accepting the position of Chair, one needs to carefully reflect on the motivations behind the desire to perform such an important, but often thankless, duty. Although both the process and the outcome can be immensely satisfying, it is important to realize that the Chair does not fully control the negotiation. She can set the tone, guide the conversation, and dictate the pace, but it is the dynamic between the delegates, which she can help manage, that ultimately determines the outcome. If you do accept the baton, use your entire repertoire of skills and personal experience to help you fulfill your role as Chair. If you are funny, use your sense of humor to alleviate a moment of high tension, if you like to cook, bring some food to the table, if you like to sing … well, sing. Like the delegates around the table, the Chair has an enormous responsibility, and the individual in that role can make all the difference to a multilateral process.

The art of chairing conferences: lessons learnt[3]

by Ambassador Tommy Koh

Tommy Koh is Ambassador-at-Large at Singapore's Ministry of Foreign Affairs. He served as Singapore's Permanent Representative to the UN in New York, concurrently accredited as High Commissioner to Canada, from 1968–1971, and again from 1974–1984, concurrently accredited as High Commissioner to Canada and Ambassador to Mexico. He was Singapore's Ambassador in Washington from 1984–1990 and Chief Negotiator of the US-Singapore Free Trade Agreement from 2000–2003. He was President of the Third UN Conference on the Law of Sea from 1981–1982 and Chairman of the Preparatory Committee for and the Main Committee of the UN Conference on Environment and Development from 1990–1992. He served as the UN Secretary-General's Special Envoy to Russia, Estonia, Latvia and Lithuania in 1993. He has also been a member of three WTO dispute panels, two of which he served as Chairman.

Introduction

I wish to distil some useful lessons from having chaired two of the most challenging conferences convened by the United Nations (UN): the Third UN Conference on the Law of the Sea (UNCLOS) and the Preparatory Committee for the UN Conference on Environment and Development (UNCED) and the Main Committee of the Conference itself (the Earth Summit). I hope that some of these lessons will be useful to colleagues who may have the opportunity to chair other major international conferences.

Lesson No. 1: Master your brief

It is not possible to be a good chairman of a conference if you do not master your brief. By this I mean mastering the rules of procedure of the conference as well as its content. This is not easy to do as most conferences have a long and complex agenda. Some items on the agenda may also be highly technical. During the conference on the law of the sea, for example, I had to understand and be able to make good judgements on such matters as the financial terms of mining contracts, the geomorphological structure of the continental shelf and margin, the life cycles of different species of fish, etc. In order to increase my knowledge and that of my colleagues in the conference, I requested some of my friends in the non-governmental organisations, to arrange briefings, workshops and retreats for us by acknowledged experts in those areas. The lesson is that the chairman of a conference must be sufficiently knowledgeable so that he is able to guide the negotiations and make good compromise proposals, if the need should arise.

Lesson No. 2: Use your bureau

Every conference has a bureau. If the bureau is small, the chairman should use it as the steering committee of the conference. If the bureau is large, as was the case of UNCED, the chairman should treat it as a microcosm of the conference. I did not ignore the large bureau but invented a smaller de facto bureau to help me in steering the conference. I called it the "collegium," which consisted of myself, the chairmen of the three committees, the rapporteur and the eight persons I had appointed to chair the eight negotiating groups I had established. At the Earth Summit, I invited the chairmen of the regional and interest groups to join the expanded collegium. Both during the Preparatory Committee and at the Earth Summit, in Rio de Janeiro, I would meet with the collegium every day. At the same time, I kept the large bureau reasonably happy by meeting with it at regular intervals and submitting all procedural proposals for its approval. If I had not done so, there would have been a revolt by the bureau against the collegium. The chairman of a conference has to reconcile the competing needs of democracy and efficiency.

Lesson No. 3: Work with the secretariat

All international conferences are serviced by a secretariat. Not all secretariats are of the same quality. However, my philosophy is to work with the secretariat. I regarded the secretariat as my strategic partner. The Secretary-General of UNCED was the remarkable Canadian, Maurice Strong. Twenty years earlier, I had helped Maurice Strong to prepare for the 1972 Stockholm Conference on the Human Environment, of which he was also the Secretary-General. From March 1990 till June 1992, I worked in tandem with Maurice Strong, Nitin Desai and the other members of their able team. I invited Strong, Desai and other senior members of their team to join the daily meetings of the collegium. I kept no secrets from them. There were no tensions or conflict between Strong and me, unlike Strong's relationship with the UN Secretary-General, Dr Boutros Boutros-Ghali. Maurice Strong was good with the media and I was happy to let him be the public face of the Earth Summit to the world.

Lesson No. 4: Be a team player and team builder

A good conference chairman must be a team player and a team builder. Those who like to work alone or to work in secret should not aspire to chair conferences. A chairman will not succeed in his enterprise if he is a solo player. As a conference chairman, you are the leader of a team. The other members of your team are the chairmen of the committees of the conference, the rapporteur of the conference and the head of the secretariat. Both during the Preparatory Committee and at the Earth Summit, I was constantly talent-spotting. I was looking for able men and women, from all the regional and interest groups, to whom I could delegate part of my responsibility. I established eight negotiating groups and appointed eight able colleagues to lead them. However, if they failed to deliver, I did not hesitate to replace them. If the negotiations on a specific text hit an impasse, I would ask the interested parties to meet under the chairmanship of one of the intellectual leaders of the conference. In every case, they succeeded in finding a compromise text.

Lesson No. 5: No secret negotiating groups

The UN has 192 Member States. Most international conferences are attended by all the Member States of the UN and sometimes, even more. It is difficult to conduct negotiations with so many interlocutors. It is, therefore, always tempting for the chairman to set up a smaller negotiating group. One should always resist this temptation unless one has the blessings of the plenary to do so. During the fourth and final session of the UNCED Preparatory Committee, the Committee requested me to take over the negotiations of the text of the Rio Declaration of Principles from the chairman of the Third Committee. I agreed to do so on the condition that the negotiations be conducted in a group of 16, eight each from the Group of 77 and OECD. The plenary agreed and the 16 members of the negotiating group were chosen, not by me, but by the two interest groups. We completed our negotiations in two days and the result of the small group was subsequently ratified by the plenary. In Rio, all the negotiations were conducted in the presence of all delegations. It was hard, but we succeeded in negotiating and adopting by consensus, the 500 pages of Agenda 21. My advice to conference chairmen is to avoid setting up small negotiating groups in secret. Why? Because the secrecy will be exposed, the product of the small negotiating group will be repudiated and your credibility will be destroyed.

Lesson No. 6: Create an inclusive, transparent and orderly negotiating process

It is the responsibility of the conference chairman to create, with the approval of the conference, an inclusive, transparent and orderly negotiating process. The process must be both transparent and inclusive in order to have legitimacy. The process must be orderly in the sense that there should be a rational structure linking the different negotiating bodies and a hierarchy of accountability. The conference chairman is both the master planner of the negotiating architecture and the commander-in-chief. He has to hold every conference officer to account. However, he is the captain of the ship. He must hold himself accountable to the plenary of the conference for the fate of the conference.

Lesson No. 7: The importance of timing

In negotiations, as in life, timing is very important. A conference chairman must intervene when the time is ripe. If he intervenes prematurely, he will be rebuffed. During the first session of the UNCED Preparatory Committee, the Committee was very polarised and could not even agree on the agenda. After an all-night session, some time in the early hours of the morning, the exhausted delegates asked me to make a compromise proposal. With the help of about a dozen colleagues, representing the different regional and interest groups, I was able to draft a compromise proposal, which was adopted. During the fourth session of the UNCED Preparatory Committee, the chairman of the Third Committee put forward a compromise text of the Rio Declaration. Although it was a good proposal and he meant well, he had acted prematurely. The Group of 77 rejected his proposal and accused him of being biased in favour of the developed countries. I had to take over the negotiations from him. The lesson is that a good conference chairman should be skilful in judging when the conference is ready to accept a compromise proposal from him.

Lesson No. 8: The quest for consensus

The decision-making process of most UN conferences is by consensus. The concept of consensus means adopting a decision in the absence of any objection. A conference chairman must work very hard to garner support for a proposal and to seek to accommodate all those who have legitimate concerns or objections to the proposal. A proposal is usually revised many times until all such legitimate concerns have been taken care of. What do you do if you are faced with one solitary delegation which is determined to block the adoption of the proposal? If you think that the delegation has a legitimate concern, you should try to accommodate that concern. However, if you judge that the delegation is acting unreasonably, you must have the courage to confront that delegation. At the fourth session of the UNCED Preparatory Committee, Israel was the only delegation that opposed the adoption of the Rio Declaration of Principles. At the Earth Summit, Saudi Arabia insisted on deleting the whole chapter, on Climate, from Agenda 21. I overruled Israel and Saudi Arabia and requested them to challenge my ruling, which I was prepared to put to the vote. They were angry, but declined to challenge my ruling because they knew that they did not have the support to overturn my ruling. What is the lesson? The lesson is that a conference chairman must be patient and fair, but he must be prepared to be firm and, if necessary, ruthless when confronted with a solitary delegation which is determined to block consensus.

Lesson No. 9: How to deal with the NGOs

Both during the conference on the law of the sea and during the UNCED preparatory and negotiating processes, I had a positive relationship with most of the representatives of the accredited non-governmental organisations (NGOs). Several of the representatives became my good friends. During UNCLOS, there was a group of NGOs which called themselves the Neptune Group. I worked very closely with them. Through their good offices, I was able to obtain the expert advice of MIT on the financial terms of mining contracts and the advice of leading American oceanographers on the continental shelf and margin, etc. During UNCED, I was very close to a group of NGOs, which put out the Earth Summit Bulletin. The bulletin was an accurate summary of the various negotiations which took place on the previous day. What is the lesson learnt? It is that, wisely used, the NGO community can be very helpful to a conference and to its chairman. However, if not properly managed, the NGOs can have a negative and disruptive influence on a conference.

Lesson No. 10: Qualities of a good chairman

To succeed as a conference chairman, one should be humble and respectful of all his conference colleagues. He should treat all colleagues fairly, whether they represent big or small countries. He should be transparent and trustworthy. He should be a good listener and be willing to take into account the interests and concerns of all delegations. He should be pro-active in reaching out to the various regional and interest groups. He should be optimistic. He should be calm, especially when faced with a crisis. He should have courage and be prepared to confront those who are determined to block progress and isolate them. He should be a good mediator and bridge builder. Ideally, a good conference chairman should be able to unite his colleagues and inspire them with their common vision.

31 May 2010

Notes

1 Tommy Koh, "The art of chairing conferences: lessons learnt," in *The Tommy Koh Reader: Favourite Essays and Lectures* (Singapore: World Scientific, 2013), 238–244.
2 I. William Zartman, "The Timing of Peace Initiatives: Hurting Stalemates and Ripe Moments," *The Global Review of Ethnopolitics* 1, no. 1 (2001).
3 Republished with permission from Ambassador Tommy Koh.

7 Mitigating asymmetric power: The 800-pound gorilla and the fearless ant

Large UN Member States can demand a lead role in multilateral negotiations; at times, others de facto yield these countries or large groups that role. Although an enlightened use of such power can produce positive outcomes, this imbalance also has the potential to negatively affect the tone of a negotiation, as well as undermine the perceived legitimacy of an eventual agreement.

"Large" in this sense can be dependent on context, and is related to such factors as political influence, economic power, historical role in the world, population, and geography. Additionally, whether and how a large country or group "controls" elements of a negotiation depends not just on a delegation's size and strategy, but also on the individual negotiator. A seasoned negotiator immediately realizes that this lead role can be both a boon and a burden (despite entrenched beliefs among some that controlling a negotiation is always desirable). It is important that negotiators operating from a stronger position understand that they should not – and in reality cannot – dictate the terms of a negotiation; that would be more akin to unilateral foreign policy, not multilateral diplomacy.

Likewise, smaller countries should not default to larger countries, assuming they will take the lead; after all, with the opportunity to have a voice on the world stage comes a responsibility to act, regardless of size. Smaller countries – and their individual delegates – also have some distinct advantages over larger countries and their representatives, which is helpful to secure and leverage.

In situations of asymmetric power, large and smaller states can suffer from false diagnoses of the other's perspective; this can further misunderstanding and muddy the waters in a negotiation. For example, large countries may feel that their smaller partners – in "abdicating" to them – are freeloading, and they would prefer instead that others speak up. Meanwhile, smaller countries may feel so "dictated to" by larger partners, that they see themselves as pawns in a larger game being played by the giants. This is not a dynamic helpful to a functional multilateral forum.

This chapter explores the impact of asymmetric power in multilateral negotiations. It highlights the challenges and opportunities that come with relative size and negotiation strategy, offering insights into how countries can leverage

the benefits of being perceived as more or less powerful, while avoiding the pitfalls that can accompany those roles.

A game changer in the climate change negotiations

The 17th session of the Conference of the Parties (COP17) to the UN Framework Convention on Climate Change (UNFCCC) in Durban in 2011 provides an example of the power smaller countries have when they band together. After weeks of intense negotiations, a draft containing information on a deal made between the "gorilla" delegations – the big and powerful economies in this case – was leaked to delegates. The "gorillas" had agreed that negotiations for a future climate agreement (now known as the Paris Agreement) would begin in 2015 and enter into force in 2020. The deal effectively delayed the start of the negotiations by four years – though many other countries affected by climate change saw the need for the negotiations to begin urgently!

When smaller developing countries – the "ants" for our purposes – found out about this closed-door arrangement, they came together in an unprecedented manner to confront the "gorilla" delegations. This cross-regional, temporary alliance between "ants" – the Small Island Developing States (SIDS), the Least Developing Countries (LDCs) and many Latin American and African countries – substantially changed the outcome of the Conference. The final draft outlined that the "Agreement" needed to be finalized by 2015 and enter into force in 2020. If the smaller developing countries had not come together, the Paris Agreement in its current form would not exist.

The march of the ants: the challenges and benefits of being small

The creature most feared in the Amazon jungle is neither the tiger nor the anaconda, but the ant. When these jungle ants act in packs, they are an unstoppable force. In multilateral negotiations, some overlook the individual weight of smaller countries and their ability to drive action on the world stage. However, when these countries unite as a common front, as they did in the Durban Climate Change Conference (see example above), they can achieve results even greater than their sum. The raison d'être of many groups created in the context of the UN, such as the Group of 77 and China, the Alliance of Small Island States (AOSIS), and Landlocked Developing Countries (LLDCs) has been to use their combined strength to advance common goals (see more on this in Chapter 4). Moreover, despite the challenges associated with relative size, even an individual "ant" can alter the dynamics of a negotiation. In certain circumstances, an "ant," armed with the insight and ability to use all of its available resources, can rival a "gorilla." Below we explore both the challenges and opportunities of being an "ant" in UN negotiations.

Challenges

Being heard

When representing a smaller country at the UN, it can be difficult for a delegate to make her voice heard – let alone be influential. She also does not necessarily have a standing invitation, unlike representatives of large group delegations, to the essential back room and behind-the-scenes meetings we discussed in Chapter 5, where issues are resolved and agreements are hammered out; instead, she needs to earn the invitation. Moreover, a smaller country's voice may be constrained by political, economic, or security interests with a larger ally or partner; it may also be lobbied by a large delegation to speak, or even keep quiet at meetings to serve the latter's interest. For example, during a formal debate on a particularly sensitive topic at a UN forum, some developing countries took the floor, drawing the surprise of others as they usually did not speak up at, or even attend, these meetings. Some of them later shared privately that they had been lobbied by a "gorilla," to whom they had close political and economic ties, to speak in support of the latter's position at the meeting.

Influence

Related to being heard is the issue of being able to influence the negotiation process and the outcome. Representatives of smaller countries, for a number of reasons, can face challenges influencing the agenda and substance at the UN. Although it is indeed a universal forum, and every UN Member theoretically has a voice, the reality can be more complex. Smaller countries may not have the armies of officers or the abundance of financial and other resources in their arsenals necessary to persuade other Member States to align with their priorities. Those countries with the ability to pay more (e.g. to UN budgets), or show up in greater numbers, or yell louder, by virtue of their financial, military, or political prominence, tend to have more influence.

Capacity

Many of the challenges associated with being from a smaller country, including voice and influence, are linked to capacity. Smaller countries, particularly from the developing world, often do not have embassies in capitals across the world. They have smaller delegations, less staff overall, and potentially more modest budgets. This can have an impact on their ability to collect information – locally and in capitals – and on their ability to communicate and message their goals. It affects the strategies available to them and the timelines within which to pursue them. It also increases their burden in that each delegate from a smaller country is responsible for so much more – be it gathering information, participating in meetings, building relationships, or achieving her country's objectives.

This is evident especially when a smaller country adopts a more prominent role, such as joining the Security Council as an elected member. For the Security Council, the larger, more powerful members have a veritable machine of staff and resources in place for such a role, not to mention the years of experience and records for those who are permanent members of the Council; they also receive very useful information sent from their embassies and networks all around the world. This puts smaller countries with limited staff and resources, relying primarily on secondary sources of information, at a particular disadvantage. This is why groups and alliances are so important in many venues (see Chapter 4).

Even countries some might perceive as "large" participate in burden-sharing. For example, Canada, Australia, and New Zealand often work together. Canada and New Zealand supported Australia when it was elected to the Security Council in 2013 and the three regularly split up coverage of resolutions in the Second Committee during the annual General Assembly sessions.

Opportunities

For the reasons above and more, a negotiator from a smaller country has to rely more on her personal repertoire of tools to make her voice heard, persuade others, and have an impact. In our time negotiating at the UN, we have seen more than a few "ants" in action who have been more than successful in doing so. The "ants," individually or in groups, can be unstoppable.

Individual negotiators from smaller countries can possess more power – and enjoy more ability to influence outcomes – than might be apparent at first. There are many benefits to representing a smaller country, especially as "ants" can be nimble, less visible, and determined.

Flexibility

A negotiator representing a smaller country can have more freedom to define (or redefine) her reputation and the perception of her country than she might if she hailed from a larger country that receives additional scrutiny and has a fixed reputation. A delegation from a larger country (the United States, for example) comes accompanied by a load of baggage with respect to reputation and perception. In comparison, smaller country representatives may have more space to characterize their agenda, interests, and approaches. For example, if a smaller country chooses not to send a representative to a key meeting on the UN calendar (be it for lack of interest, or because it does not want to speak up on a sensitive issue on the meeting's agenda, or any other reason), it is likely to be given the benefit of the doubt by others when it uses the excuse that it does not have the personnel capacity to do so; if, however, a "gorilla" country were to do the same thing, it would more likely be read as disinterest or even disdain for the process.

Neutrality

Smaller countries sometimes do not have strong views on all the issues at stake in a negotiation; this could be because it does not have the capacity to give attention to all the items under discussion; it has calculated that it is not worth expending too much of its precious political goodwill to negotiate some of the less vital issues; or it may truly not have an interest in some of the subject matter. Regardless, this neutrality or lack of interest in the issue allows a negotiator more room to help craft creative compromises and take more of a problem-solver or leadership role. It is probably not by accident that UN Presidents of the General Assembly often appoint the Ambassadors of smaller countries to co-chair negotiations at the UN (e.g. the Ambassadors of Kenya, Hungary, and Ireland co-chaired the negotiations on the 2030 Agenda, including the Sustainable Development Goals, while Namibia, with the support of Bangladesh, introduced the first text on women peace and security, the watershed UN resolution 1325).

Autonomy

For delegates of some smaller countries, their relationship with their respective capitals may be less rigid than that for delegates from larger countries. Larger countries may have a desk devoted to every issue with an officer who cares about the nuances of every debate. As a result, they believe (sometimes correctly, sometime erroneously) that they have a responsibility to delve deeply into every item in a negotiation; their negotiators must carry the water (as the idiom goes). This can be a burdensome constraint. A less rigid oversight structure can free delegates to undertake additional creative problem-solving and strategic relation-building. Likewise, a representative from a smaller country can take the floor at times with less scrutiny from her capital, local civil society groups, and local media, as they may not have the bandwidth to keep watch on every intervention made at the UN.

Determination – the unglamorous beginning of the Sustainable Development Goals (SDGs)

There are many articles detailing the SDG process (see footnote if you want to learn more).[1] This is an abridged version focusing on one of the main actors involved in the process.

In 2011, the UN was starting to discuss what would come after the end of the Millennium Development Goals[2] (MDGs) in 2015. While most delegates favored an MDG-plus agenda, meaning just adding a few more targets to the existing goals, Paula Caballero, a diplomat from Colombia had a crazy idea. The new goals should be universal, not only for developing countries; it should also have a greater focus on sustainability, she thought. She was also of the view that the goals should be applicable to all countries, instead of only to developing countries. These ideas were significantly different from the MDG-plus agenda that was cooking in New York.

She discussed this proposal with high level officials in her capital, where she received their full support. Paula then discussed the idea for these "sustainable development goals" with a few of her friends in New York (two of the authors in the book included). During her first two years of shopping around the proposal, most delegations thought that the idea would never fly – it was too "outside the box" – and they disregarded the idea. Paula, nevertheless, persisted with her vision. She traveled the world, visiting capitals, went to every imaginable conference, and each time she gathered more support. Guatemala, the United Arab Emirates, Peru soon joined the proposal. Little by little, the "SDGs" became a more attractive option, and there was overwhelming response by countries to participate in the Open Working Group on the Sustainable Development Goals.

The story of Colombian Paula Caballero's proposal on the SDGs (see above) underlines the power of the individual to substantially change an outcome on the world stage. If Paula had been from a larger developed country, with more entrenched interests, a larger bureaucracy, and greater economic commitments, her idea might have been rejected by her capital, at worst, or viewed with more suspicion by other countries, at best. Yet, there she was, a woman from the developing world, persisting – at all costs – in communicating this new proposal. It is worth noting that Paula had the support of her capital as this was essential for her to carry on her outreach efforts, despite the criticisms that came with challenging the status quo. Paula forged a group of cross-regional allies, first from her own group the G77, such as Guatemala, Peru, UAE, and many others, and then from the developed world. Together, this group of smaller developed and developing countries pushed the idea forward and made the SDGs a reality.

Strategies

In our experience negotiating at the UN, the "ants" were often the change makers in a negotiation. They were certainly the bridge-builders and the creative problem solvers. They were able to make things happen, sometimes when no one else could. To fully leverage the opportunity inherent in being an "ant," and to have greater impact on any negotiation, we suggest the strategies below.

Act as a bridge

Serve as a neutral broker between delegations, or between groups, that have very different points of view on an issue. By making proposals that would help parties achieve a compromise, you can not only help the negotiation process, but also become noticeable to the point that other delegates voluntarily seek out your opinion. An example of this strategy is delegates who bridge the north–south divide in a negotiation and are able to speak to key actors on polarized sides of the debate. Chairpersons of negotiations also like to bring on board bridge-builders in their behind-the-scenes negotiations to help breakthrough stalemates and find solutions. In acting as a bridge, you gain a voice and influence (see Chapter 6).

Safety in numbers

Try not to act alone. Form alliances with friends and foes alike (see Chapter 4), which will allow you to build those bridges and sell those creative ideas. It always helps to have a support network, across the spectrum, backing you up.

Take-on a leadership role

In multilateral negotiations where there are multiple sessions taking place in parallel, groups struggle to find lead negotiators to represent their views in the different meetings. By volunteering to coordinate the position of the group and to speak for the group, your voice is amplified and your influence is strengthened. Likewise, chair a meeting. Visible leadership roles will increase your voice and influence.

Speak up

If you have something to say, be among the first to take the floor. Delegations can then refer to your statements (voice), you will set the tone of the meeting (influence), and other delegates will notice your confidence (both). This also helps to earn you invitations to subsequent behind-the-scenes discussions as the organisers will know you are able to contribute to the discussions.

Think outside the script

Once you know the ropes of the negotiation and the issue well, don't be afraid to propose the unimaginable if you believe it can bring about good change. If being creative will not negatively impact your country's other priorities, dare to do it.

An "ant" can win (and be a "gorilla," too)

Former Colombian diplomat Juanita Castano told us the story of her tactics during Security Council debates on a proposed embargo on Iraq after its invasion of Kuwait in 1990. The majority of the permanent members of the Security Council wanted an embargo to punish Iraq for its aggression; the non-permanent members opposed it because of its impact on Iraq's population, particularly the most vulnerable.

As the debate dragged on over hours, and pressure from the permanent members mounted, only Colombia continued the debate against the embargo – an "ant" against the "gorillas." Finally, threatening to walk out of the room, which would have ended the debate and blocked any decision (all Council members must be present for a session to continue), Juanita gained the full attention of the "gorillas." She used the rules of procedure to shift the power balance, winning exceptions to the embargo for basic food items and for children. She felt in this case that, as an "ant" delegate, she needed to become a "gorilla."

The perception of the 800-pound gorilla

The old expression about the 800-pound gorilla is used to describe someone – or something – that just comes in and takes over without regard to norms. It likely stems from the old joke, "where does an 800-pound gorilla sit? ...

anywhere it wants! Haha." At least that is the version we learned as children. Regardless, it is a reference to power disparity.

A power disparity between countries can occur for a number of reasons, such as political or economic influence, geopolitical history, or size, either in terms of geography or population; it becomes manifest in multilateral negotiations when others perceive – rightly or wrongly – that a country or group has surplus power in some realm. A "gorilla" is born. This perception of power disparity can be further exacerbated by the strategy, attitude and actions of the "gorilla" delegation in the negotiation, and even more so by the behavior of the individual negotiator representing the "gorilla" delegation. Regardless, the perception (or reality) that one "gorilla" delegation is dictating, controlling, or holding hostage a negotiation can greatly impact the process, dynamics, and content (and potentially the legitimacy) of the outcome. Such potential dominance, if misused or abused, can eventually impact the efficacy of a multilateral institution as well.

Gorilla burden ... and opportunities

Sometimes a delegation becomes a "gorilla" just because it is seen that way – it is large and powerful in a number of realms and is just expected to lead (or take over). This certainly happens to the United States whether it means to be a "gorilla" or not, as well as to some of the larger negotiating groups. This can be both an opportunity and a burden.

Burden

The expectation that a "gorilla" will take the lead in a negotiation can put additional pressure on the "gorilla" negotiator, as delegates defer or even default to her to "do the right thing" or "hold the position." Often, others don't even feel the need to speak up as they expect the "gorilla" to fight the fight for them; at times, they hide behind the "gorilla" negotiator and let her play the bad guy. This can be exhausting for the "gorilla" negotiator, and, unless agreed beforehand as a strategy among allies to achieve a good outcome, can feel unfair. It also makes for an unbalanced and seemingly one-sided negotiation: Why was that one negotiator speaking up all the time? Did no one else care? Or agree? Or have a view? One of us cannot count the number of times that other capitals depended on her to be the bad guy in the negotiation, because they knew the United States either had to have it, or would just say no. So, although there was support for the U.S. position in the room, no one felt the need to speak up. They wanted the United States to be a "gorilla." It is an unpleasant, lonely position to be in.

Opportunity

In contrast, the expectation that a "gorilla" will take the lead in a negotiation can also be an opportunity for the "gorilla" negotiator to be at the frontlines of constructing a meaningful outcome that will benefit the greater good. How the "gorilla" delegate uses this expectation is what makes all the difference. If the de facto lead listens, creatively proposes solutions, and tries to bring thought and meaning to the discussion, this can alter the tone and dynamics of the negotiation for the positive. This approach, however, takes effort. It is significantly more difficult to be constructive than just accepting the role of bully and proceeding like one. Being the "gorilla" is an opportunity to lead by example and for the "gorilla" delegate to be the multilateral actor she would like to see in others.

Gorilla by demand

A delegation may regularly choose to act as the "gorilla" in a negotiation as a strategy to achieve its goals, insisting on concessions and holding the negotiation hostage to its demands. This is a regrettable short-term approach to multilateralism. Occasionally, a delegation may believe it has to act like a "gorilla" out of necessity. For example, domestic considerations may push a delegation to behave as a "gorilla," seizing power regardless of size; in such cases, a delegation has calculated that its domestic concerns are more important than its multilateral relationships and it is willing to bear the cost for the potential fall-out. Regardless of the reason, we maintain acting as the "gorilla" is never a good approach if there are viable alternatives. Being a "gorilla" by force in a negotiation can encourage other delegations to put on their "gorilla" suits as well. It generally also does not win a delegate – or delegation – friends and allies. Delegates who often use this strategy can be seen as bullies, and treated as such, with fear and disdain, but little real respect, making it more difficult for them to achieve their delegations' goals the next time. While it is still possible to produce a good outcome via this approach from time to time, e.g. the "gorilla" delegation's position may be one that produces an outcome that is truly best for all (this is remarkable, but it can happen), we don't recommend the "gorilla" as a negotiating strategy if there are other options.

Gorilla by personality ... or insecurity

The "gorilla" approach – or tone – can also originate with an individual negotiator. Typically, these negotiators represent a "gorilla"-appearing delegation and for some reason (either tactical or philosophical) have decided that they must "win" and will seek to dictate the terms within which to do so. "Gorilla" delegate behavior manifests in an unwillingness to compromise, a demand that others concede, and in speaking louder and more often than other delegates; basically, it is bullying. Such an approach is the trademark of an insecure negotiator who feels she cannot achieve her delegation's goals in any other way. As we noted above, a delegate may get what she wants using this method in one negotiation, but she will not gain friends and allies for the long term. We therefore don't recommend this method, with one exception: a thoughtful

negotiator can tactically resort to the "gorilla" approach in a negotiation with intractable delegates when it is truly necessary to reach a fair compromise.

Counteracting the imbalance

The point of the UN is to empower all of its Member States to have a relevant voice in global policy. This requires large states and smaller states to cooperate towards outcomes acceptable to all. The behavior of a "gorilla," either intentional or accidental, can act to disempower others, undermining this goal. If an outcome is coerced, bullied, or dictated, it can lose support or legitimacy; when no one except the "gorilla" feels good about an agreement, it is unlikely to be a success. Large countries or groups should not want smaller delegations to feel powerless; likewise, smaller delegations should not offer their power and voice to "gorillas." Both actions defeat the purpose of multilateral efforts.

Delegates from "gorilla" countries need to develop an awareness of the potential impact of their relative power on the dynamics of the process and the efficacy of an agreement. These delegates can counteract the negative effects by devoting themselves to a number of behaviors. Although we have already introduced some of these in discussing what makes a good negotiator, the following are especially important for "gorilla" delegations:

- *Set the tone*: Display a willingness (even eagerness) to find mutual solutions, making it clear that you sincerely want a positive outcome, despite differences.
- *Cooperate*: Work cooperatively with others behind the scenes and clearly express your desire and willingness to do so, publicly or privately, as appropriate.
- *Listen*: Really listen to other delegations and then make proposals that – in maintaining your position – show you have heard or are responding to others' statements.
- *Be polite*: Be respectful and responsive. If you are a native speaker, be judicious on linguistic corrections (while making sure the document makes sense!).
- *Shut up*: If you are a big delegation, the less you talk to achieve your aims, the better. If someone else makes your point, regardless of delegation, agree succinctly and then stop talking. If you know another delegate will say what you need to say, wait for her to do so, and then chime in if necessary, but never hog the floor.
- *Let it go*: There is no need to fight over every minute point (unless your instructions dictate that you must, and then you should have a chat with your capital). Don't nit-pick the details (aka don't make the perfect the enemy of the good) and choose your battles wisely, allowing every delegate to feel she has gotten something.

The gracious use of influence

As we noted earlier, the U.S. delegation is often perceived – and sometimes behaves – as a "gorilla." One negotiator with whom we have worked is particularly attuned to the impact of her status. Former U.S. Ambassador to the UN's Economic and Social Council, Elizabeth Cousens, shared with us the following advice:

> *While negotiations are about give and take and finding the highest point of common ground, they are also about power – use it with precision and unless it's the last negotiation for your country or your career, think about whether you're saving or squandering your capital for future rounds. The gracious use of influence or weight is almost always more effective than bullying.*

Other delegations liked working with Ambassador Cousens in UN negotiations because she set an inclusive tone – she listened, she spoke thoughtfully and responsively, and she worked with others, without ceding her priorities.

The above points assume the absence of a spoiler or an intractable delegate. If one of these is present, use your "gorilla"-ness wisely, in coordination with your friends and allies (and even opponents), to counteract the problem delegation. This is the only reason for a "gorilla" to ever accept the role of the jerk in a negotiation; it is otherwise just not necessary.

It is difficult for delegates from smaller countries or groups to counteract a "gorilla," short of becoming "gorilla"-like themselves. We don't advise this, as it creates a never-ending loop of "gorillas," as each delegation returns to the next negotiation angrier and more "gorilla"-like. The most effective means to combat a "gorilla" is to forge a relationship with the "gorilla" delegate and informally take her aside, work with her, and, if helpful, explain her impact on the negotiation. The Chair can attempt to do this as well. Alternatively, either a delegate or the Chair could speak to the "gorilla" delegate's head of delegation about the behavior and its impact. Additionally, a delegate can point out, in an intervention in the formal negotiation, that one delegation appears to be holding the process hostage, as a means to draw more public attention to the issue. However, these last two approaches also risk escalating the problem. Use your judgment in your attempts to get to the best outcome.

Conclusion

The UN, particularly the General Assembly, exists as a venue for global policy, where every Member State that has a seat at any given table has a voice in that conversation. The UN has power to the extent that every Member State feels it can have an impact on the UN's outcomes. This is unique and allows burden-sharing of the decision-making process and also ensures buy-in for the implementation of the outcome. It also enables leadership not just from "gorillas" from whom it might be expected, but from unlikely suspects, such as smaller countries. The diminution of these voices by a "gorilla's" word or deed can undermine the purpose of the UN and its effectiveness; global partnership suffers.

The importance of UN venues is often also in their existence: just having that conversation in that space matters, even if delegates are only place-holding for a subsequent higher-level conversation or an eventual decision. And when the attention of the world turns to that item, or when Member States are finally ready for action on that matter, the venue is there, the partnerships are there, the relationships are there for the conversations required to tackle that crisis. We believe the importance of this cannot be overstated.

Besides, "gorilla" bullying is the mark of an immature negotiator; forcing others into an agreement will ruin your reputation and relationships. Like too many things, it all basically boils down to the golden rule, "treat others as you would want to be treated." So, regardless of your role, be it a "gorilla" or an "ant," don't sweat the small stuff in a negotiation. Remember that we all have the responsibility to act wisely, a responsibility that comes with the privilege of being given a voice at the UN. Work your hardest to get agreement on the most important components of an outcome, and to protect your interests, while making sure everyone has a say. As delegates, we are all actors on the global stage and we all deserve to be heard. You, the negotiator, have the power to make this happen. You matter as much as – or more than – your flag.

Notes

1 Kamau Macharia, Pamela Chasek and David O'Connor, *Transforming Multilateral Diplomacy* (London: Taylor & Francis Group, 2018); David Donoghue, Felix Dodds and Jimena Leiva Roesch, *Negotiating the Sustainable Development Goals: A Transformational Agenda in an Insecure World* (London: Taylor & Francis Group, 2016).

2 The MDGs emerged from the Millennium Declaration and other intergovernmental agreed outcomes in the 1990s. The MDGs are a set of eight goals and 21 targets that primarily cover socio-economic issues such as extreme poverty, maternal health and education. The span of the goals was from 2000 to 2015. The MDGs primarily focused on the basic needs of developing countries.

Part Three

Working on It

8 I am a female negotiator: so what?

When I was a child, I never thought that being a woman could prevent me from achieving whatever I wanted in life. It certainly did not, and I'm privileged for that. However, I'm sure that the price that I paid to pursue my goals – the price I still pay – is higher than the price that a man pays. Why? Because I feel that there's a need for women to constantly prove their worth, and that requires an extra amount of perseverance.

Being a young woman diplomat at the UN was a huge challenge for me. The first time that I participated in a Group of 77 (G77) and China meeting I thought: "I will never be able to do what my colleagues do," "I'm not prepared for this," "I can't articulate an argument to fight with them," "these people will never listen to what I have to say." But I tried hard and spoke once, and then again and again, until people started paying attention to what I was saying. I finally became part of the conversation. It took time and required an understanding of the dynamics of the negotiations, knowing my colleagues, working with both their and my preconceived ideas, but it was amazing how much I learned, how it opened my mind, how it made me grow.

I remember that one time, when I was coordinating a meeting, a male colleague who clearly opposed the women's rights agenda requested the floor, just before a female colleague did. When the male colleague noticed this, he indicated that he wanted to let the female colleague speak first. I told him: "No, no, I believe in gender equality, if you are first you are first, that is what we mean when we speak about equality." I hope he understood that what I wanted for myself, and for every woman, is fair treatment, not special privilege, not to speak first. What I pursue is to be valued for what I am and not be excluded because of my gender. No more and no less.

A woman diplomat from Latin America

As a global society, we are coming to realize that – for a variety of reasons and in a number of meaningful ways, across cultures, geographies, and sectors – the typical experiences of women are often very different from the typical experiences of men. This holds true as well in the context of UN negotiations. Because of this truth, we felt that a book about negotiating at the UN written by three women needed to, in some way, speak to this reality.

Rather than drawing on generalizations from literature, or relying solely on our own experiences to be representative, we reached out to the female colleagues with whom we have had the privilege of working over our years in multilateral negotiations; we asked for their perspectives, their stories, and their experiences. These female colleagues come from diverse cultural backgrounds, which helped shape how they perceived themselves at the UN, and likely also how they were perceived by others. From the excerpts we received, it is clear that – although attitudes and behavioral differences are certainly accentuated by cultural norms and individual characteristics – there remain common elements that make a woman's experience in UN negotiations different from that of a man.

In the narrative and anecdotes below, except where noted, many of our female colleagues have chosen to remain anonymous; some are acknowledged at the end of the book, whereas others asked not to be named at all. Regardless, we think that the anecdotes we have received, and the lessons they convey, speak for themselves in presenting what it means to be a female delegate at the UN.

Different treatment: equal, please, not special

Although this is changing, men have historically far outnumbered women in multilateral negotiations. A 2016 article from UN News lends some insight into the plight of the female Ambassador, much of which is familiar even for diplomats negotiating at lower levels.[1] The article cites the number of women

ambassadors at 37 out of 193 Member States (less than 20 percent). As we have noted throughout this book, the composition of the delegates seated at the negotiation table – along with their relationships, experiences, preconceptions, and biases – dictates the dynamics and tone of a negotiation.

Partially as a result of their historic scarcity, and as the anecdote that opens this chapter makes clear, women can be treated differently from men in multilateral negotiations. Though always a form of sexism, sometimes the different treatment is helpful, but misguided (as in the anecdote that opens this chapter). As another example of this, in the run-up to an important conference, one of the co-chairs of the process told the U.S. head of delegation that his two lead negotiators – both female – were "charming and cooperative." Although he meant it as a compliment, he would never have referred to a male delegate in this way. At the same conference, the nickname among male delegates for an all-female team negotiating ocean issues was "the mermaids." The epithets were all meant affectionately, of course, but none of them were precisely appropriate in a professional setting. Again, women just want to be equal, not special.

Sometimes the difference in behavior – or sexism – is less positively intentioned. A European colleague shared her story of a UN Security Council negotiation, in which a male delegate – in an attempt to demonstrate that her argument was not convincing – explained in his intervention that it is scientifically proven that women work from their emotions and men from reason, so women could therefore make no rational arguments. He intended this to stop debate on the issue, and expected the point to be conceded to him; it wasn't. There happened to be a number of women in that UN Security Council negotiation, none of whom took kindly to a non-fact about women as a negotiating tactic. These women immediately overcame the differences between their positions to create an intra-group block in solidarity with the female delegate who had been attacked, isolating the offending male delegate.

Unintended innuendo

Working in the Security Council, where I covered UN Peacekeeping Operations in Haiti and Afghanistan, was a huge contrast to the Second Committee, in which I worked years later. At the Security Council, the room was 14 men and me; all the secretariat staff were men too! Outnumbered, I just had to dig deep, be very prepared, not take charming comments at face value, and think quickly for comebacks. I was young (mid-twenties), less experienced, single, and social: though potentially a good combination for relationship-building, it was also an opportunity for contact-making to go the wrong way. This was in 2004, before many of the current conversations about behavior in the workplace began, and my efforts to build consensus over coffee were completely and utterly misread by my male negotiators. An invitation from a male counterpart to go out for drinks to discuss a negotiation was even more loaded; while it might sound fun and can be effective to break down misunderstandings, back then, going – or not going – sent strong, and sometimes wrong, signals to male negotiators. Going could be interpreted as interest beyond the professional; not going could mean that I was either not "fun," or not dedicated enough to the job. I often ended up embarrassing my counterpart and myself; it was sometimes quite awkward.

A female U.S. negotiator

Female negotiators who shared their stories for this book wrote about men's attitudes towards women negotiators having cultural aspects; that said, many noted that more respectful treatment did not necessarily come from men representing more developed countries. Some male delegates just treated every delegate equally, while others clearly reacted or interacted differently based on gender. One delegate shared that "some men were just out of touch": for example, with a straight face, a representative of the Holy See once rejected a proposed amendment from a female delegate as being "too paternalistic."

A female colleague from a Middle Eastern country shared that a male delegate from a developed country responded to one of her interventions with a horrible racist comment; she didn't know whether he was misogynist or xenophobic, but she straightened him out in her next intervention and he apologized. Irish delegate Denise McQuade shared the following:

> The only time I experienced outright sexism was when a colleague from a developing country, in the middle of a rather heated discussion, asked me if I had children and, upon hearing that I didn't, suggested that this was the reason I was so upset. His ongoing unprofessional behavior was the reason I appeared angry.

Argentine delegate Josefina Bunge told us of a negotiation during which a male Chair ignored her requests for the floor. She was sitting next to another female negotiator who, when she saw what was taking place, requested the floor as well; the Chair ignored both of them. Both women eventually asked a male colleague to request the floor and then to pass it to one of them. The male delegate was granted the floor before either woman; on taking the floor, he said that Argentina would speak instead, and gave his female colleague the floor. In addressing the Chair, she made a point of the situation, remarking that she "hoped it did not have to do with gender issues or discrimination."

On this subject, Egyptian Ambassador Dr. Namira Negm writes,

> I am not sure if it would have been different if I was a male negotiator, but I believe the answer may be in the affirmative ... behavior towards women,

> it has nothing to do with regions, because even men from supposedly broad-minded societies may still try to intimidate women with looks or comments. In the Arab and African Groups for example, it was the opposite.

She continues that she was often the only female in the groups working on legal issues, and that her male colleagues "respected me and most of the time sought my guidance because they trusted in me and my professionalism"; however, when there were negotiators from capitals, it was more difficult for her because they "had conservative backgrounds and were uncomfortable negotiating with women."

Attacks can appear (or even be) personal

A pregnant delegate to the UN Conference on Sustainable Development was negotiating a paragraph on reproductive rights in the outcome document. Her delegation felt strongly about the issue and the national position was to be proactive on reproductive rights wherever possible in the text. One delegation (through a male delegate) chose to emotionally attack her delegation during formal negotiations, calling her Minister a "murderer" during a small group discussion. Meanwhile, a female representative from a non-governmental organisation (NGO) supporting the delegation's position told the delegate she was "the wrong person to be negotiating" this issue ... because she was pregnant! The delegate, to her credit, took it all in stride and unemotionally soldiered on, winning an acceptable outcome for her delegation (and in the delegate's own words, "a win for women's rights!"). Both the male delegate and female NGO representative made this negotiation more emotionally charged than it should have been, as well as needlessly personal – because the delegate was a pregnant woman and they had preconceptions about what that should mean.

It appears that a small percentage of male delegates still fail to see women professionally, believing they cannot reach out to them for fear it would be misconstrued – by the female delegate or their mutual colleagues – as a date. A female delegate from Asia reports that she shocked a male colleague in 2017 by being friendly and professional enough to ask him for coffee in order to better understand his position; he admitted he would never have approached a female colleague to do the same for fear of it being misread. Although norms and perceptions have evolved over the years (see anecdote above, "Unintended innuendo," from 2004), some remain nervous of sending the wrong message, which can have an impact on relationships and – ultimately – on equal treatment.

Misconceptions about women abound, resulting in treatment different from that a man might receive in the same situation. Be it positively or negatively intended, the difference in treatment is sexism. It is also an issue that can negatively impact the negotiation – slowing down progress, making compromise more difficult, and generally undermining the process. There is hope, however. Our Argentine colleague who shared her story added that the Chair who ignored her apologized; they are now good friends and – to her knowledge – he has never repeated his mistake.

Twice as prepared ... for bias

One negotiation that stands out was a Philippines-sponsored General Assembly resolution on "Women and Climate Change," during which there was a very heated exchange between the female delegate from the Philippines chairing the negotiation and a male delegate from another G77 member country. The male delegate appeared unhappy about the discussion, and was particularly displeased to be talking about "women's issues." (And having to walk more than five city blocks to the meeting in the rain likely didn't help.) He did not oppose the resolution, but challenged almost every line, arguing to weaken language or remove whole statements.

The Philippines' proposed text focused on the specific needs of women due to climate change impacts on rural livelihoods, maternal health, and other issues. It included a specific reference to a radio information campaign aimed at rural women on farming in a changing climate, including preparation for possible water shortages, extreme heat, or pest infestation. This was an uncontroversial matter for others, but the male delegate challenged it, saying in a heated way, "Why would she need this? Her husband will be doing all the work anyway!" The Philippine Chair calmly and matter-of-factly reminded him that such knowledge is critical to women's survival; she cited statistics about male urban migration (which leaves women running farms) affecting his continent, and said the language was non-negotiable. The delegate challenged the chair, but then relented, and left the negotiations in a huff. He was replaced by his junior colleague who remained silent for the rest of the meeting. It appears that the delegate – and not the delegation – had a problem with the discussion. The Philippine Chair subsequently noted that she had to be twice as prepared to manage someone from a supposedly like-minded country.

In addition to having to work harder to achieve a good outcome, the Chair – and her supportive colleagues – had to fight for the resolution itself. Such fights have been a long-standing struggle at the UN, as women's issues, including access to sexual and reproductive health and reproductive rights, are very political topics provoking intensely controversial debates.

A female North American diplomat

Proving themselves: women have to work harder

Most of the female delegates that shared anecdotes with us conveyed that women had to work harder in negotiations, both to earn respect and to prove their competence. Further, they found that this applied to the opinions of both male and female colleagues. One negotiator recounted the story of her first time on a delegation with a slightly senior male delegate. Although she had two-plus years of UN experience, especially in budget negotiations, and had a good reputation among her colleagues, her senior colleague informed her that this was a new venue for her and she was to observe rather than help with the heavy negotiating load – he added that he "didn't trust" her. He also assigned an inexperienced male delegate – at his first UN meeting ever – to negotiate a rather difficult budget issue. The first-time male negotiator did not do well; after a day and a half of failed negotiations, the more experienced female delegate took over. She brought the negotiation to a successful conclusion, securing her delegation's interests and working with other delegations to satisfy theirs. Thereafter, her senior colleague trusted her. However, she had not been given the benefit of the doubt that her inexperienced male colleague had had from the beginning. Another female negotiator often felt second-guessed by a more senior woman on her delegation, despite the clear evidence that she was following instructions and the negotiation was proceeding smoothly.

Become the "gorilla"

In negotiations on a UN General Assembly development resolution, a female U.S. negotiator and a male G77 negotiator were at odds over a number of detailed issues. After weeks of protracted informal meetings, the chair of the negotiation prepared a compromise proposal, to which the United States and G77 delegates agreed with some small changes. The G77 delegate, however, broke the deal just before the resolution entered the silence procedure. This happened three times: the United States and G77 delegates would reach a deal through the facilitator, which the G77 negotiator would then break. Each time, the G77 delegate would come back to ask for more, whittling away to get closer and closer to his desired position and further from an actual compromise.

After over two weeks of this, the U.S. negotiator had had enough and knew she wouldn't get anywhere unless she made a strong statement. As she had planned to do if it happened again, she stormed out in response to the fourth round of additional demands, declaring there would be no agreement. This finally got the G77 negotiator's attention: this woman was serious. He agreed to everything from the first compromise immediately. The additional demands clearly weren't coming from his group; he just thought he could get more from a woman (after seeing him negotiate with others, our delegate assures that this suspicion bore out). Storming out was the only way a woman negotiator from the United States was going to earn his respect. And it worked. (A word of advice, however: use only in extreme circumstances; no one likes an actor).

Ntesang Molemele, a female negotiator from Botswana with extensive UN experience in both New York and Nairobi, shared that she worked very hard to negotiate a good outcome for her delegation on a groundbreaking resolution at the UN Environment Assembly, spending months "researching, lobbying, persuading." Of her experience, she said:

> At times, I had the impression that this is still a man's world – one delegate insinuated that I was "aloof" and "not cooperative"; one woman diplomat once told me that the problem with me was that I liked "arguing with men!" It was not the first time that such phrases and techniques were used to try to suppress my voice. There were times I felt some people were too timid to voice support for my position, although they did support it, for reasons I still don't understand. One time, I had to inform certain delegates that I've been working in the multilateral realm since the beginning of my career in the foreign service and demonstrate to them that I have in-depth knowledge. But my experience has taught me that, indeed, the world of diplomacy is still highly chauvinistic and women are held to different

> standards than men, as if women should give our ideas to men, and have them present them on our behalf.

Some also felt that women from developing countries had additional challenges to overcome. For example, Ambassador Dr. Namira Negm from Egypt shared that diplomacy is a tough job for women, especially for those women from more traditional societies, where men are perceived as superior to women and it may be poorly viewed for women to travel alone or seek professional achievement. She writes,

> in the UN, depending on which negotiation one is involved in, the attitude of colleagues will differ. A new female delegate from a developing country – unless she appears quite confident – may not be taken seriously and her interventions may be ignored. In my first month at the UN, I had to make it clear, during a debate on an aspect of the Vienna Convention on the Law of Treaties, that I carry a PhD in international law and that I know exactly what I am talking about. After that, the coordinator of the negotiations, who had been dismissive, had a change in attitude, and was attentive to everything I said.

A female delegate from the Caribbean shared that:

> Working both at the UN in New York and in UN Framework Convention on Climate Change negotiations involved challenges that occurred because I was relatively young, a person of color, and a woman from a developing country. I had the impression of consistently being ignored until I asserted myself and established that I actually knew what I was talking about. I always felt that I had to work harder than others just to be viewed as a potential equal. This dynamic was the same, both within and outside of the G77 and China; the UN in general can be very male dominated. I definitely think that even as a young person of color from a developing country, if I were a man and not a woman, I would have had less of a difficult time gaining the respect of colleagues.

She recalled being consistently ignored throughout drafting sessions in one committee, whether she sought clarification or proposed solutions. The Chair of the committee pushed agreement on the text against her objections and sent it to the Plenary, where it became clear that his language was overly complex and unworkable – points she had made repeatedly during the session. When she approached the Chair with a solution that finally saved the text, he was shocked, "staring with a look you would give a dog that suddenly spoke." After that he was still condescending but slightly less dismissive of her input.

Juggling

> *I enjoyed my five years as a negotiator at the UN very much, though it was a struggle during those years to balance my personal life. I arrived in New York with a seven month old baby and gave birth to a beautiful girl a year later, all while my country held the G77 Presidency and I was the coordinator for the Second Committee. Later, while I was a G77 coordinator for green economy in the "Rio+20" negotiations and on debt issues, agriculture, and food security in the Second Committee, I felt torn apart between juggling work commitments and motherhood, and more often than not felt that neither my kids nor my job were getting my best.*
>
> Argentine delegate Josefina Bunge

Internal barriers: self-doubt and hesitation

A number of women negotiators who spoke to the authors of this book noted that they felt some lack of confidence, or insecurity, about their knowledge and abilities, especially as they began their time at the UN. They felt this may have held them back. Others noted that they felt more comfortable being absolutely sure about their statements before they intervened, whereas they noticed men did not hesitate. One Chilean negotiator wrote:

> When I look back at my time at the UN, I remember feeling unsure of myself. Some of my male colleagues from my own mission – with basically the same training and instructions – didn't seem to be as affected. I have since learned that women tend to be less likely than men to step forward unless they are very sure of what they will bring to the table. I wonder if this held me back from taking on challenges that may have taught me much but that seemed out of reach, and if I would have approached this differently if I had been aware of it.

Another female delegate wrote that throughout her time at the UN, she perceived that women generally "did not intervene as often or as forcefully as men; they hesitated more before speaking." The same negotiator also felt that women "did not always project confidence on the level of that exhibited by their male colleagues." In *Lean In*, Sheryl Sandberg refers to such internal barriers to success being linked to confidence and perceived expectations.[2] However, for women, projection of confidence can be a double-edged sword: becoming too aggressive or being perceived as too powerful can imperil likability with certain types of negotiators and impact ability to build coalitions. As Sandberg writes, "aggressive and hard-charging women violate unwritten rules about acceptable social conduct" because "success and likeability are positively correlated for men and negatively correlated for women."[3]

On the subject of women's confidence and its role in their success, Ambassador Negm wrote:

> I believe also that the individual personality of the female makes a difference in the negotiation context. When a female is strong enough and confident in what she expresses, she is less apt to any type of intimidation. On the contrary, she can be the cause of intimidating the others she is negotiating with. In the UN and any multilateral negotiations, it is all about perceptions. If a woman is perceived serious in her work and she masters what she does, anyone thinks twice before approaching her inappropriately, be it through the use of condescending language, harassment or intimidation.

Views: female negotiators on themselves

A number of our colleagues shared stories of their collaboration with other female delegates in negotiations; in some instances, these partnerships had a huge impact on their UN experience and were immensely helpful to their success. A female Indonesian negotiator noted that she was "very lucky to have female friends, to ask for guidance and assistance in bridging divides between different groups." Female Irish delegate Denise McQuade shared that:

> in the Second Committee in general, but especially as the WEOG[4] member of the Bureau, you need a network within the G77 if you want to get things done. While mine wasn't exclusively female, I enjoyed excellent cooperation with a number of female colleagues – these were the people I turned to when I wanted to know what was taking so long and needed ideas for how we could fix it.

Support and shared commitment

> *On a daily basis, as a female diplomat, I am the only woman at the table; at best, I am one of two women in the room. This could be a meeting with host government counterparts, a visiting delegation from my own government, or with business sector contacts. It is always startling to me that, even in 2018, there are so few women in diplomacy. There are a handful of female role models, but it can be lonely. This is a stark contrast from my time negotiating with the Second Committee on sustainable development. There, we had much more female representation – not parity, but more than one at the table! The reason this is important, as I learned immediately from my time as a negotiator, is that women form natural bonds, no matter which position they are arguing. So fewer women at the table at least meant I could be part of a ready-made and often close-knit*

alliance, whether on process (i.e., are we going to be talking all night) or substance.

Process is so important when negotiating multilateral documents: starting on time, respecting the Chair, ensuring all papers and proposals are shared ahead of time. I and many of my female colleagues had lives to get home to – whether it was just trying to get to the gym, put the kids to bed, or get to a volunteering responsibility – we had a common understanding on efficiently moving the discussion along. (It often did not seem to me that many men were on-board with this agenda.)

On substance, my female colleagues and I could often agree quickly to a shared opinion and a mutual outcome. We also often knew each other's red lines or no-go points and could work quickly to find a suitable outcome, where everyone got something they wanted. We were more flexible, trusting, less conniving, and had significantly less ego. I truly believe all the women were there with a shared positive objective. We also worked on a divide and conquer approach: we would devise a strategy to meet other colleagues ahead of time, recognizing who had a bond with whom, to have a shared approach prior to the start of the negations.

A developed country diplomat

The Chilean colleague who shared her initial insecurity also highlighted the following about support from other women and a sort of "female approach" to negotiations:

> There was a positive side to my uncertainty. Because I was somewhat unsure, I tended to approach negotiations by trying to get as much information as possible by talking with others one-on-one. I relied on other women negotiators I trusted and respected and would regularly ask their views and opinions (on everything!). The information I tended to have was pretty thorough and that was a plus when reporting back to my capital and giving feedback for further instructions. I made some very good friends I could work very closely with, even if our countries' views differed on particular issues.

A large collection of research has begun to demonstrate – in addition to differences in the way that men and women are perceived and treated in the workplace – there are differences in the "typical" behaviors and approaches of men and women in work settings. Some of our colleagues found this to be true at the UN as well. A French colleague told us that she found female negotiators to be more positive, more forward-looking, and less arrogant than their male counterparts. She felt that, as women, "our pragmatism helps us build coalitions, which is key in the UN." Interestingly, a 2016 *New York Times* "Upshot" piece summarizing the research on how women govern differently from men supports these observations. The author states that "the biggest differences appear during behind-the-scenes work," where women "interrupt less (but are interrupted more), pay closer attention to other people's nonverbal cues and use a more democratic leadership style," which allows them to "build coalitions and reach consensus more quickly."[5] As we discussed in Chapters 4 and 5, coalition-building and behind-the scenes work are strategies crucial to successful negotiated outcomes.

Similarly, our co-author Rebecca shared that, in her experience, women who were most effective in negotiations "were confident in their quest to find solutions to issues, which attracted confidence from others; in some cases, the confidence was not necessarily personal, but more related to their mission or objectives." She felt they were knowledgeable, resourceful, and trustworthy, which allowed them to partner and strategize with others; in her view, they tended to be problem solvers.

Many female colleagues felt that women had a significant impact in negotiations, regardless of any additional challenges. For example, Urawadee Sriphiromya, at the time of publication Thailand's Chargé d'Affaires a.i. in Manila, shared the following:

> During my term in New York, I was in charge of the Second Committee and later the Security Council and the General Assembly. The years 2009–2012 were marked by the aftermath of the global financial and economic crisis and the shaping of the post 2015 global development agenda leading to the Rio+20 Summit in 2012, which launched the process to form the current Sustainable Development Goals. As part of the G77 and China, I took part in numerous negotiations that were significant to the lives of people, especially in developing countries. I had the privilege of working with several strong ladies in the group from various parts of the world, who were very vocal and most of the time succeeded in amending the texts or defending the proposals. I found that the work of the G77 and China and the Second Committee highly benefited from the perspectives of these woman negotiators. The results of these two years of negotiations with strong women negotiators paved the way for the Post 2015 Development Agenda and the adoption in 2015 of the Sustainable Development Goals that aim at leaving no one behind.

Similarly, our colleague from Singapore, Yu Ping Chan, wrote, "Did I feel that being a woman negotiator made a difference? Perhaps – mainly because I think that many women negotiators are dedicated to multilateralism, persuasive particularly under pressure, and persistent to the very end!"

Gender influence: using all the resources at your disposal

Some delegates also shared stories about using the perceived differences, preconceptions, and biases to their advantage. They noted that men do it, so can women. It is a question of using all the available resources to their best advantage. Here are some candid stories:

Use the perceptions

Another pregnant delegate shared that (in happy contrast to the example above) her main contact on the Vatican delegation was very solicitous; he got her a chair, and chocolate, and offered her the most forward-leaning reproductive rights language her delegation had ever seen from the Holy See.

Make yourself approachable, and beyond reproach

One negotiator used her family to make herself more approachable and less threatening, to male and female delegates. She invited groups of delegates – sometimes strategically, when she felt they needed stronger relationships – to her home for dinner or out with her and her husband. Another female colleague remembers that a male negotiator from a particularly conservative country brought his charming wife to social outings and invited delegates annually to his home for a BBQ with his family; including family in work events is rare among male UN delegates, she said, and it improved trust and friendship with some of his female colleagues.

Use the bias

One female delegate from a developed country wrote:

> I think, as women, we have all had to jockey – or posture a bit – in negotiations with a male colleague in order to allow him to perceive that he has also scored a point when we did, or that we conceded (whether we did or not) when he made a concession. I quickly learned that this was important for many male delegates, independent of their country of origin. I have played a little stupid in negotiations, many times in order to avoid offending a male negotiator, and twice (that I can remember) to be able to get any deal at all with a male delegate. I never had to do this with a female colleague. I will also note there were many male delegates that did not require it.

Our colleague Denise McQuade shared the following:

> I served at the Irish Mission to the UN from 2005–2010, covering a variety of sustainable development and humanitarian issues. While I rarely experienced any outright discrimination as a female negotiator, I certainly think people underestimated me at times. While this can be irritating, it's not really a disadvantage! There were certainly occasions where despite having made Ireland's position very clear at the outset, colleagues seemed surprised when later in the negotiations I put forward proposals – in the guise of a compromise – that went a long way towards reaching Ireland's goals.

One female negotiator said she witnessed another female delegate delicately flirting her way through nearly every negotiation with male counterparts, extremely effectively and without unintended consequences. She was otherwise "constructive, honest, fair ... and clearly creative!" Another single female delegate noted that, after years of working closely with a male colleague, she was often surprised to discover later that he was married with children. This happened a number of times, and every time the "he" in question had behaved, though not inappropriately, as if he were unencumbered – not rushing off after negotiations to be home, going out late, flirting playfully. Clearly, it's not just a female tactic.

Biology matters

A number of developed country delegates sent stories about traveling to negotiate while they still had nursing infants at home. A UN meeting schedule can be brutal in such situations. Several remember needing to regularly excuse themselves from the negotiation to pump, with Chairs who were more or less understanding; another brought her baby, who embarrassingly cried through the opening Plenary. We have discussed above some of the impacts of being pregnant in a negotiation. Then, there is the delicate issue of bathroom needs. Our co-author, Rebecca, remembers a distinguished and venerable female Ambassador from Uganda, who deftly chaired a number of negotiations in which she participated ... and who ensured regular bathroom breaks by calling every two hours for a brief "biological break." Rebecca is thankful both for her chairing skills and those breaks.

Harassment

A number of delegates alluded to harassment from male colleagues during their time negotiating at the UN. This ranged from inappropriate jokes or glances to targeted and offensive behavior intended to coerce or intimidate. One delegate shared, that

> *a male colleague who I had worked with professionally over several months asked me one day to a quiet room, on the pretense of discussing work, and he tried to kiss me. I was appalled, not only because I was happily married, and I stayed clear of this delegate for the rest of my term at the UN.*

Unfortunately, in this realm, the UN is no different from many other professional settings.

Negotiating is hard for everyone, man or woman

While several female negotiators felt strongly about there being a distinct difference in the way men and women negotiated, others felt less strongly about any difference. Kartika Handaruningrum, of Indonesia, shared that she generally had support from more senior diplomats from G77 countries, many of whom were also female diplomats; she felt there were many strong female role models who had a significant impact on the work of the UN in New York. Kartika continued:

> As for myself, I never felt discrimination or as if I had additional challenges as a female negotiator from a developing country. Women have equal footing at the UN and female negotiators form close bonds that go beyond that of mere colleagues, as we had the same amazing experience of serving in New York.

Another Asian female negotiator put it this way:

> I honestly don't know if my negotiating experience would have been significantly different if I was a male negotiator. I worked very hard in my job, as did my male colleagues, and never found myself unfairly treated in a negotiation due to being a woman (maybe I was just oblivious!). I forged good working relationships with male and female negotiators alike; similarly, I have had difficulties with both male and female delegates in particular negotiations. Yes, I felt insecure at times in the negotiation room, but I knew male negotiators who were plagued by their own self doubts. There have been occasions where I noticed I am the only female negotiator at the table amongst male Caucasian colleagues. In such cases, I have never felt out of place due to either my difference in gender or race, nor have I tried to modify my behavior for the circumstance. It is true that having left the UN, I call my female negotiator friends on the phone more frequently than my male negotiator friends. But I subscribe that to our mutual love for fashion and common concerns about mothers-in-law!

Other lenses

Some of the female negotiators that shared their stories with us noted that gender wasn't the main prism through which they viewed the negotiation dynamics; other lenses, such as race or being from a developed or developing country, seemed to come to the fore. As an Asian female diplomat wrote,

> *Since my college days in the US, I have become much more aware of my race; more specifically, I consciously ask whether I will be discriminated against because of my skin color. When I walk into a negotiating room these days, the first thing that strikes me is not whether I am the only woman in the room, but whether I am the only non-white person in the room.*

Former Colombian diplomat Juanita Castano said:

> *I was Deputy Permanent Representative of the Colombian Mission to the UN in New York from 1990–1993. Those four particularly tense years gave me deeper insight into the political problems of the world. The problems that the developing world faced at that time, and we still face today, were so deep, so unfair, and had so much historical background, that I had no time to discern whether being a female negotiator gave me a stronger or weaker position. I just had to be tough and tougher, because more important than being a woman, was the fact that we were the developing world, and I was negotiating on behalf of that world.*

Dewi Wahab, a senior official at the Ministry of Foreign Affairs of the Republic of Indonesia, who has served in the multilateral realm for a decade, made a similar point as follows:

> I must say that being a woman was not an obstacle to being a negotiator or a facilitator. Perhaps the challenge was more about the substantive issue and the politics among the Member States, including navigating your country's interest. For example, in the case of an Indonesian resolution on food security, the challenge was to adopt it by consensus and with operating paragraphs that would have real impact on the ground, while balancing the interests of the various groups of member countries or individual countries involved in the negotiation. In the case of a resolution I facilitated on climate change, the challenge was more on balancing the pressures by the big economies against the interests of countries who were feeling the impact of climate change.
>
> And sometimes, honestly, perhaps being a woman, I felt I was obliged to live up to certain principles, while in reality, the UN negotiating context was full of politicking (be it getting stabbed in the back from your ally or having somebody speak badly about you to achieve their own interests). But if you put these obstacles aside, the challenge that every negotiator faces is the same – it is about ensuring that your integrity is intact, because you needed trust and it did not come just like that; you needed to earn the trust. So I can say that it was a real challenge to become a negotiator in the context of the UN in New York, but if you can do it, it is very satisfying because not only do you contribute to your country and the world, but you get to know good friends and good people during the process.

Summary

This chapter is another testament to the fact that the individuals taking part in a negotiation play a large part in dictating the negotiation process and outcome. The individual in the room matters, as do the dynamics between those assembled. A negotiator should do her best to adapt to any culturally-dictated, socially-inept, or gender-inappropriate attitudes diplomatically and without losing a sense of what she represents and what her delegation is hoping to accomplish; there is always a difficult actor or circumstance, and an experienced negotiator – male or female – rolls with the punches, to the extent reasonable. That is diplomacy. At the same time, female negotiators are rightly calling for equal treatment, challenging stereotypes and behaviors that are no longer acceptable in the workplace. We hope to continue to see progress on this at the UN and in every realm.

Notes

1 "Feature: A conversation with female ambassadors about the UN Security Council," *UN News* (17 March 2016), https://news.un.org/en/story/2016/03/524642-feature-conversation-female-ambassadors-about-un-security-council.
2 Sheryl Sandberg, *Lean In: Women, Work, and the Will to Lead* (New York: Alfred A. Knopf, 2013), 27–28.
3 Ibid.
4 Western Europe and Others Group.
5 Claire Cain Miller, "Women Actually do Govern Differently," *The New York Times* (10 November 2016).

9 Please excuse us as we upgrade our process … and software

Earlier in this book, we discuss some of the problems with the system of negotiating resolutions at the UN, especially during the General Assembly. This chapter focuses on ways to improve the process. Namely, (i) reduce the number of resolutions tabled each year and bring more focus to each resolution; (ii) encourage a culture of innovation; and (iii) provide more training for negotiators. This chapter also discusses a number of ways in which new digital technologies have had an impact on multilateral negotiations.

Improving the process

Reduce resolutions; increase focus

The third week of September is when the new General Assembly session begins each year. More than 250 General Assembly resolutions are negotiated and adopted from the start of the session through December. This can be extremely challenging for countries with small delegations to the UN. More significantly, it raises questions about the amount of time and resources UN Member States can devote to negotiating each resolution and ensuring that they are of the highest quality, e.g. clear recommendations that catalyze action and account for implementation challenges.

Currently, General Assembly resolutions on most topics are negotiated at the UN annually or biennially, sometimes multiple times in the same year, and in multiple venues. This creates "resolution fatigue," where countries are less likely to pay attention to the issues in the resolution because they are featured too frequently – sometimes, so frequently that no developments of note have taken place since the last resolution. In many cases, less frequent treatment of most topics would make them more meaningful in terms of the content reflected. Delegates are also not able to focus on the priority issues of the moment because there are too many other standing resolutions (items requiring annual review as a result of the statutory requirements of subsidiary organizations) competing for attention. Consequently, the international community lacks clarity on the issues on which it should focus amidst the sheer number of resolutions being tabled. The UN's ability to efficiently and effectively tackle important issues is ultimately jeopardized and its relevance comes into question.

Instead, UN Member States should amend the periodicity of each resolution so they are tabled less frequently, e.g. every three to five years. This will enable delegations to conduct more detailed research and analysis on the issue being negotiated, and determine national priorities to achieve more meaningful results. It will also reduce the number of resolutions at each General Assembly session. This will give negotiators more time to produce more coherent resolutions that better reflect Member States' intent as well as send clearer messages to the international community, offering more insight into the pressing global issues that the UN has prioritized and enabling it to galvanize support for these issues accordingly.

To change the periodicity of resolutions, UN Member States must, together, exercise political will. Anything else could be detrimental for the UN's relevance in addressing today's global challenges. If each country argues against changing the periodicity of its resolution because that is the country's pet issue, other countries will be encouraged to do likewise. At the same time, delegations need to maintain a consistent position across venues: if a Member State's Second Committee delegate argues for biennial reporting from an UNGA subsidiary body, the Member State's delegate to the subsidiary body in question needs to fight the same battle.

UN Member States also tend to add their pet issues to resolutions, like hanging ornaments on a tree. Although adding a paragraph on a particular issue to a resolution can draw the international community's attention, these paragraphs often remain in future iterations of the resolution (usually at the insistence of the Member State that introduced it, or another that has adopted the pet issue). The tree is now so cluttered that visibility of any one ornament has been drastically reduced.

Take for example, the annual resolution on *Oceans and the law of the sea*. At the 55th session of the General Assembly, the resolution adopted had 47 operative paragraphs. At the 60th session, five years later, the resolution had 114 operative paragraphs, more than double the number; at the 70th session, it had 328 operative paragraphs, almost tripling the number in 10 years. Once something – anything – is introduced at the UN, it is nearly impossible to get rid of it. This is because of a pervasive belief among most delegates that if something is removed or not mentioned, it is unimportant. This mistaken notion needs to be debunked.

When a resolution has been adopted, UN Member States should accept that the items or paragraphs in the adopted resolution are relevant in the short to medium term. If so, there is no need to reiterate the same item or paragraph in future iterations of the resolution unless the item or paragraph needs to be updated, corrected, or re-enforced. Re-enforcement should be done extremely selectively, or it will open the floodgates for all pet issues to be re-enforced, regardless of their value. For example, future iterations of the resolution on *Oceans and the law of the sea* should focus on new developments without repeating most of the previous resolution; a brief reference to the document number of the previous resolution can also help enable nothing to be lost. A more concise resolution will offer the international community insight into the current priority issues and the new proposals. Further, clear, considered, and targeted resolutions significantly benefit the implementation process and can better galvanize support for the recommendations in the resolutions. A final word on brevity – lengthy resolutions lead to tired negotiators (and bored readers), not necessarily better agreements.

Encourage innovation

Another way Member States can improve the UN is by encouraging innovation. To maintain relevance, the UN needs to keep up with changes in today's world. However, for negotiators working at the UN, familiarity is the fall back, trumping change every time. Every year, UN Member States expend precious resources on UN negotiations, which are all too often discussions on items that have long since lost relevance. Many phrases are re-introduced or inserted in resolutions just because "they were there before." Negotiators also tend to treat new ideas suspiciously. Some Member States are so suspicious of the UN and anything new coming from it that their general mandate to their negotiators is to babysit old items and squash anything new. Delegates should, instead, reward creative approaches that can improve the UN negotiation system, and sell these ideas to their capitals. Everyone has a stake in making the work of the UN as meaningful and relevant as it can be.

Take for example negotiations on the 10 Year Framework of Programmes on Sustainable Consumption and Production (SCP) in 2011. Lead negotiators from the Group of 77 and China concluded that the language in the preambular section of the Chair's negotiating text was either captured in the operative section or had little additional value on its own. As they only had two weeks to negotiate the Framework, the Group of 77 and China agreed not to lose valuable time, energy and goodwill negotiating the preambular paragraphs within the group as well as with the developed countries. Instead, they focused on the operative paragraphs, which described the heart of the SCP framework, such as its objectives, structure and implementation.

When negotiations on the text began, the experienced Chairperson from Australia also suggested that the negotiations begin with the operative section, and convinced all the delegates to agree to this approach. After UN Member States had concluded negotiations on that section, it was evident that the preambular paragraphs were not necessary and all delegates agreed to their deletion. Ultimately, the negotiators benefited by expending time and energy only on the most relevant text, and the international community gained a more concise and coherent SCP framework. UN delegates should thus encourage innovation that can improve the system of negotiating resolutions at the UN, including ways to focus on areas where there is additional value.

Another example of using creativity to add value in diplomacy is the approach by the WTO Dispute Panel on "United States – Safeguard Measures on Imports of Fresh, Chilled or Frozen Lamb Meat from New Zealand and Australia." At the start of the second substantive hearing on the case, the countries involved delivered lengthy statements that seemed to have little value. To move the discussions forward on the second day, the panel (without prior notice) sought the parties' views on four questions key to the case. The change of format "got the three parties away from reading scripted statements ... to think on their feet, to engage each other and to focus on the issues."[1]

Training

Government representatives sent to negotiate resolutions will be more effective if they are trained to protect their equities while working towards fair compromises that will result in better outcomes for the international community. Member States should instill in their negotiators the idea that they are a part of a problem solving team working together to send a message to the world. Although they represent their countries and compatriots, like any representative, it is their responsibility to achieve the best outcomes for their side within the greater context of the best global outcome. This will better enable negotiators to move beyond the motions of negotiating the same resolutions and settling on the lowest common denominator. With more training, negotiators will understand the advantages of spending more time exploring each party's interests in order to brainstorm win-win options.[2] It will also empower negotiators to adopt resolutions that (i) add value and catalyze positive change; (ii) are implementable; and (iii) are clear on priority global challenges so that stakeholders can focus on solutions.

Because of its large membership, the breadth of stakeholders, and the fact that just one country can block consensus on a resolution (in many venues), the UN is a particularly challenging negotiating forum. Government representatives need to be trained in building alliances, forging agreements across North–South divides, and finding win-win opportunities under tight time and resource constraints that will benefit all parties. Although tutorials in the structure of UN negotiations are important, simulation exercises are essential in helping delegates grasp the dynamics. By experiencing what it is like to negotiate a UN resolution, negotiators will see how easy it is to excessively rely on "agreed language" from previous resolutions or to settle on the lowest common denominator just to close the deal. More importantly, they will learn what it takes to overcome such UN negotiation "habits."

Negotiation training through simulation exercises based on the UN also demonstrates to government representatives how to look beyond countries' bargaining positions to core interests, as well as how to recognize certain types of negotiators and their styles. Having a first encounter with a "spoiler" negotiator who is negatively influencing the negotiation process in a simulation rather than a real negotiation can make all the difference to a real outcome later. With government representatives better trained to negotiate UN resolutions (and read their colleagues), UN outcomes and the negotiation system itself will be significantly improved.

Technology and negotiations

Technological advancements – and debates about them – are ubiquitous across sectors and societies. Digital technologies especially have the power to fundamentally alter, in ways both good and bad, the manner in which business is conducted in almost every sector; in many areas, it has already done so. This is true as well for multilateral negotiations, where digital and other technologies are already having an impact. Many interactions and processes at the UN benefit from the use of digital technology; there are also areas where traditional tools of negotiation still hold value.

Online vs. offline

When one of us stepped into a formal negotiation room after some months away, she was surprised by the quietness of the room – where was the usual scurrying on the sidelines by delegates to bridge differences, share proposals, and exchange information? When she asked a younger colleague, he replied, "isn't that what WhatsApp is for?" WhatsApp and other online messaging tools now allow delegates to seed ideas to others almost incognito. This can be a good thing if the seeder is trying to be constructive but cannot do so openly due to country interests or otherwise. Group texts also arguably make it easier to keep allies and your own delegation informed quickly. The downside to such tools is they advertently or inadvertently exclude others. Previously, when you saw key players huddle together, your antennae would go up as this was a sign that something was cooking. If you were bold enough to join the huddle, you might be able to pick up what they were considering and how that might affect your interests. With some of these conversations having moved underground, it can be harder to pick up intel; it can also be harder for newbies to fit in and be included in existing group chats.

With the quality of video chats quickly improving and with parties now being able to view and edit an online document together, there may be pressure – due to efficiency and economic considerations – to reduce face to face negotiations going forward. For example, interested parties can come together via these online tools to make progress on outstanding issues between formal negotiating sessions at the UN. This can speed up the negotiation process. It can also save time and money from having to fly in delegations from their home countries, thereby reducing carbon emissions as well!

That said, face-to-face negotiations are important in themselves, and ultimately irreplaceable for building and using real relationships. There is just no other way to truly build trust, or even just humanize your counterparts. The Durban climate change agreement was on the brink of collapse, when the EU Commissioner for Climate Action Connie Hedegaard stepped in and clinched the deal. The game changer was Hedegaard getting up from her seat and crossing the conference room in the middle of a tense formal negotiation session to speak to India's Minister of Environment and Forests Jayanthi Natarajan on a possible solution. As both ladies spoke – visible to all the other negotiators – more key players left their seats to gather around this important informal negotiation. Hedegaard's physical (or offline) action was a powerful symbol of humility and cooperation. Such gestures cannot be reflected in the same manner through online messaging tools and it is important that negotiators do not neglect the use of offline gestures.

All in real time

At least one of us co-authors remembers the world of UN negotiations before the advent of the smart device (both phones and portable computers), when negotiators could not just write back to capital while sitting in a negotiation room for real-time guidance; the ability to do so is not always an improvement, and has made negotiations simultaneously easier and more difficult. Now that every delegate has a device connected to the Internet in front of them to consult, they are looking at them ... constantly. Attention to the negotiation itself and the dynamics in the room has diminished, as negotiators are on a device seeking input or planning the next negotiation (or playing games) rather than interacting with other delegates in the moment. Real-time advice can be the proverbial lifesaver; it has been for us. However, the associated attention deficit can contribute to misunderstandings and poor relationships – holding up progress – even as communication apps help with networking and bringing negotiators closer together.

Technology has also had an impact on delegate relations with capital (see Chapter 5). With real-time communications, bureaus at headquarters do not always feel the need to invest in the work it takes to provide thorough guidance in advance of negotiations, which can leave delegates unprepared. One of us has even worked with certain desk officers who now send no instructions at all, and want instead to be consulted on every detail of every development as it happens – either because of busyness, laziness, or micromanagement. Not only does this disempower the negotiator (in networking, speaking, making any deals), but the constant communication with the desk further distracts her from the negotiation itself. Ultimately, this makes more work for everyone, and guarantees a poorly-informed strategy for a poorly-defended position (and possibly a lost seat in the side deals and backroom and no place in the compromise).

Communication technology further allows uncertain or insecure delegates to use the desk as a security blanket. We once knew a negotiator who basically ignored her guidance, asking for permission from her desk officer every time she spoke or agreed. Separately, one of us (expert in climate negotiations) once spent an entire weekend providing guidance, including verbatim interventions, on a chat app to a delegate (who had never negotiated climate change before and was unprepared to unexpectedly do so) at a meeting across the world. Although helpful for an SOS situation like the latter example (additionally saving time and money on last-minute travel for additional delegates), overuse of this communication dynamic can also make more work for everyone. And it turns the negotiator into a mere seat-warmer (talk about a waste of time and resources!).

Social media diplomacy

To successfully implement, including ratify, a negotiated outcome from the UN, it is important that the relevant stakeholders are on board and engaged. For example, it is not sufficient for the UN Secretariat to implement the Sustainable Development Goals that were negotiated at the UN; they must be subsumed into school curricula, taken up by civil society groups, integrated into government policy and understood by the general public. Social media tools, like Twitter and Facebook, can help with some of these by boosting traction on key ideas, pushing out the narrative and rallying support. The UN has also launched Global Pulse, a platform that harnesses big data as a public good, which is working on the Sustainable Development Goals by finding out how policies are working through real-time data and further understanding the changes taking place that affect human well-being.[3]

Social media tools – for good and ill – have also influenced confidentiality and timelines in negotiations at the UN. For example, the Security Council often holds confidential meetings in the consultations room, where only members of the Council can participate. In the past, other delegations would wait outside the consultations room for the scoop. With the arrival of Twitter, WhatsApp, and other social media apps, however, the game has changed as information from the Security Council is now being leaked even before the meeting ends. At times, there is even an unspoken competition among Council members to push out their own narrative on what is being discussed behind closed doors first. It is thus much harder to maintain the confidentiality of the information shared at Security Council meetings these days, which can imperil trust – and increase discomfort – in the discussions. Furthermore, as news on the various international hotspots being discussed by the Security Council pours in from social media outlets "in real time," the Council is pressed to respond ever faster than before.

Broadcasting negotiations

Increasingly, multilateral meetings – and even some negotiations – are available for streaming, live and archived, on the internet, for anyone interested in viewing them. UN meetings that had been fairly opaque, written about only by insiders who understood the nuances, are now available for all to see. Like every other technological advancement, this change has good and bad aspects. The increase in access to the proceedings and in transparency of the processes is excellent. However, the loss of the interpretive lens can lead to problems. Without an insider's understanding of the details, public misunderstanding of the proceedings is guaranteed; UN details are not widely taught, so there is no reason to expect that someone who has not studied or partnered with the UN would understand it (sometimes even we don't!). The public display also reduces delegates' control of rumor and information – tools well-used by many delegations to get an acceptable outcome. Again, this is good for the sake of transparency, but bad for the theatrics sometimes necessary for a good deal (see Chapter 5). From this perspective, it also has a profound impact on the performance that negotiators must give. Less official – less visible – arrangements foster frankness and creativity. When all is broadcast, these suffer, as does individual trust.

Summary

The more things change at the UN, the more they stay the same; at least that has been our experience. See the "Lessons Learned and Experiences Shared" piece by former leads for the G77 and China and the EU in the box at the end of this chapter. The challenges and lessons they described in 2013 remain relevant five years later. Another key lesson shines through in their article – just because delegates represent different negotiating groups with opposing positions, does not mean they cannot work together to find common ground. This is the guiding principle for a successful UN outcome and the type of diplomacy that will change the world.

By virtue of its multiparty nature, progress will be slow, but the UN cannot remain static; without change, this essential global entity risks irrelevance. Real change – some of which must come from UN negotiators themselves – is required to address the challenges the world faces and keep the UN responsive and effective. Although the specific solutions will be different for every forum, every venue, and every grouping of delegates, opportunities for improvement are there. We urge negotiators to pursue these when they can, for the good of the institutions themselves, for the public perception of the UN, and for its impact on the world. We also recommend that delegates take advantage of the new technologies that aid, while not neglecting the key interpersonal relationships and face-to-face interactions on which good negotiations and robust compromises depend. We sincerely hope that both process and technology can improve the global outcomes that this essential multilateral conglomerate produces; we also know that everything takes time in a bureaucracy, especially one as large as the UN.

Towards an effective diplomacy for sustainable development: lessons learned and experiences shared[4]

By Ambassador Nadia M. Osman, former Chair of G77 and China, and Jakob Ström, former Presidency of the European Union for Sustainable Development

At the time of publication Ambassador Osman is with the Ministry of Foreign Affairs, Republic of Sudan and Mr. Ström is Deputy Head of the Embassy of Sweden in Amman.

Over the next few months, a number of High-Level events are expected to substantively contribute to shaping the post-2015 development agenda, and hopefully in the process, accelerate the pace of sustainable development. Among these events are the inaugural meeting of the new High-Level Political Forum on Sustainable Development; a High-Level meeting on Disability and Development, which will examine the success of Millennium Development Goals (MDGs) and other Internationally Agreed Development Goals (IADGs) for persons with disabilities; and a High Level meeting on MDGs focused on accelerating action and partnering for impact, and continuation of the negotiations pertaining to the Sustainable Development Goals (SDGs), and consultations regarding the implementation of Rio+20 Outcome Document.

As diplomats from the North and South, respectively, we see an urgent need for more effective multilateral diplomacy geared specifically toward sustainable development – an overarching theme of the opening 68th Session of the United Nations General Assembly. We base this observation on our personal experiences of facing each other across the UN negotiation table several years ago.

As Former Chairperson of the Group of 77 and China, and Representative of the Presidency of the European Union on Sustainable Development negotiations at the United Nations in 2009, we led our groups in traversing a challenging international environment marked by raging financial and economic collapse and food crises. As coordinators of developing countries' and European nations' positions, we sat through endless nightlong consultations both within and amongst negotiation groups. We led fierce confrontations and struck difficult compromises. Keeping our groups united while pursuing their strategic interests and enhancing the spirit of compromise was indeed a delicate balancing act.

In retrospect, we are struck by the convergence of our views related to the negotiation process.

As a general observation, diplomacy at the UN follows patterns that in many ways are as old as the organization itself. A number of factors have changed, however. The agenda has expanded steadily, especially with the proliferation of issues and concerns with transboundary impacts, such as climate change, desertification, loss of biological diversity, and global health issues. There is general agreement that global solutions are needed to confront these common challenges.

Membership of the UN is almost four times greater than it was in 1945. Moreover, an increasing number of governments are willing and able to express their perspectives and pursue their national interests, which adds richness as well as complexity to problem solving.

The recent proliferation of information communication technologies (ICT) has also allowed negotiators to stay in touch both with their capitals and each other, as well as to browse and share information online during the course of negotiations. ICT developments help create a better flow of knowledge and enhance transparency, yet challenge negotiators' abilities to synthesize and process such a tsunami of information in a timely manner to stay abreast of the pace of negotiations.

While the workload has become heavier and the time pressure greater, there are legitimate concerns over the slow pace of progress in negotiations and the occasional irrelevance of outcomes to real developments on the ground. Such concerns should be taken seriously and debated openly. The UN must not be allowed to deteriorate into a talk shop of little political relevance. A vigilant effort must be made to ensure effective intergovernmental methods of work if we are to bolster global solutions to common challenges – solutions which can make a difference in people's lives.

We believe this can be achieved through the exchange of experiences and focused open debates.

Based upon our own experiences, we have identified ten major "lessons learned" which we are certain, if elaborated upon and applied, can contribute to a more effective multilateral diplomacy on sustainable development, thereby leading to meaningful agreements.

1 There is a need to seek from the outset a thorough understanding of the major global political and economic developments and forces, including their impacts in shaping and reshaping international relations and national interests. These global dynamics have a direct bearing on our understanding of the negotiation climate and factors affecting it. Lead negotiators of country groups should set aside time early in the negotiation process to informally brainstorm and exchange views.
2 In 2009, building bridges between group members and between the major groups was a decisive factor in reaching consensus on many difficult issues. UN diplomacy for sustainable development is not a zero sum tug-of-war; rather, it more closely resembles a "prisoners' dilemma" where cooperation is the most difficult and yet most rewarding path to take.
3 It is of paramount importance to seek to understand and appreciate each other's interests, concerns and priorities. There must be a keen effort very early on to identify areas of convergence and divergence. We encourage negotiators to initiate discussions, first within their constituency and then beyond, before a text is drafted. There should be an attempt to generate ideas and identify directions based on common gains and interests, and then allow draft texts to follow logically.
4 Confidence building, mutual respect and establishment of trust are essential. Ample time must be set aside for dialogue, not only as a courtesy, but also to understand the complexities underpinning disagreements. Identifying common ground and where further agreement could be sought, and moving these areas forward, can generate enthusiasm and incentive and can aid in maintaining momentum.

5 More time for negotiations rarely generates better decisions but more dedication to informal preparations across divides usually does. There is no perfect resolution. Negotiators must work within a limited timeframe towards an outcome that adds value to previous agreements and at least partially addresses each party's interests. As convenient and important as it is to use "agreed language," which preserves the integrity of past agreements and the consistency in political positions, there is also the need for open-mindedness, new ideas and suggestions that seek the common good.

6 It is recommended that negotiators help their colleagues, when required, with procedures, articulation and access to information, to help level the playing field, as sometimes the lack of experience with formalities and routines can impede consultations.

7 Negotiators should seek to contribute to reinventing and reinforcing multilateralism, eschewing ineffective practices or cynical attitudes. Innovation and improvement in planning, negotiations, reporting and follow up is crucial. They should demand reports and evaluations that are relevant, readable and contain realistic recommendations that can inform collective decision-making. Deadlines for tabling drafts and concluding negotiations should also be respected.

8 The number of draft resolutions presented at the UN each year should be assessed periodically. Too many resolutions both overwhelm negotiators with work and reduce its impact through an inflationary effect.

9 In the area of sustainable development, it is important to allow time within groups and between them to share experiences regarding national relevance and implementation of decisions at the country level, such as the role of national development strategies, coordination at the country level, the role of International Financial Institutions, and the state of human and institutional development, to name but a few. Indeed one important challenge has been the lack of implementation and follow-up of decisions and agreements related to sustainable development reached after such lengthy negotiation at the UN. Dynamic exchanges of experiences, including those pertaining to challenges and solutions around country level implementation must be allowed to inform and guide negotiations if we are to make a real difference on the ground.

10 To chair a group of countries or to share the burden of negotiations on behalf of a group entails a particular responsibility with respect to outcomes. A good outcome requires a listening attitude towards both members of your own group and other players, as well as an attempt to lead your group to a compromise. The 68th Session of the General Assembly offers a multitude of issues on which all parties can secure outcomes that will improve their citizens' wellbeing.

11 Negotiators need to ensure that members of their group fully understand the evolving dynamics of negotiations and that reaching common

ground will involve sacrifices, especially in national positions. Diplomacy is a craft that can always be improved. More emphasis could be given to training, both within and across groups.

12 Negotiators must offer total respect to each party in a negotiation and allow every country to voice its concerns freely. Moreover, they should treasure emerging consensus between parties far apart and never take lightly the breach of potential agreement. With willingness to sacrifice elements of national interest, there is a real opportunity to achieve common interest, while reminding representatives of the space for oral reflection of national concerns. It is our sincere hope that these suggestions, inspired by lessons learned through our personal experiences, may encourage an open debate between diplomats and thus help improve the UN's methods of work and result in higher quality, more relevant outcomes.

Published by Outreach Magazine-Stakeholders Forum on 20 September 2013.

Notes

1 Tommy Koh, "My Experiences with the WTO Dispute Settlement System," in *Economic Diplomacy*, ed. Margaret Liang and C.L. Lim (Singapore: World Scientific Publishing Co Pte Ltd, 2011), 153.
2 Roger Fisher, Ury William, and Bruce Patton, *Getting to Yes: Negotiating Agreement without Giving In*, 2nd ed. (New York, N.Y.: Penguin Books, 1991).
3 See https://www.unglobalpulse.org/ for more information.
4 Republished with permission from Ambassador Nadia M. Osman and Jakob Ström.

Conclusion

> *The first year at the UN, I felt trapped and unable to use my voice. Once I mustered the courage to speak, I realized the enormous responsibility and power that I had in any UN negotiation. It didn't matter that my country was small; if my ideas were good and I had strong allies – by virtue of friendship more than political ties – I found that I could help shape outcomes. With a little faith in my fellow negotiators, the UN can be the mustard seed able to move the mountain that separates "us" from "them" and build lasting bridges.*
>
> *Jimena Leiva-Roesch*

When we teach UN negotiations to representatives from governments and international organisations, as well as graduate students, we are often asked if we can teach a person *to be* a UN negotiator. Our short answer to the question is yes. The skills can be learned, and we hope this book has provided you with insights; like all skills, these must be refined through practice.

Here, we summarize the key lessons we have sought to convey, in the hopes that by adopting and adapting these tools, you can better make your way in negotiations, at the UN or beyond.

Negotiating the hard stuff (Chapter 1)

- In a negotiation, a negotiator aims to secure her priorities without crossing her red lines, while building trust and goodwill with her counterparts. This includes by exuding both warmth and competence through her actions, as those perceived as such are more likely to receive help and cooperation.[1]
- A negotiator also needs to identify her counterparts' priorities and red lines, as any shared objectives are opportunities for building alliances, while different priorities and/or red lines are opportunities for making trades or creating solutions where both parties can benefit. To build confidence at the start of the negotiation, parties may wish to focus on items where agreement can be easily reached, also known as "low hanging fruit."
- Package deals can be used to encourage trade-offs, particularly if more incentives are needed for concessions to be made. However, moderates may be at a psychological disadvantage when they trade with spoilers because a

spoiler moderates her bargaining position to a lesser extent than a moderate does.

- Momentum is another psychological factor in negotiations. If most parties appear to be in agreement, the one sitting on the fence is likely to be less inclined to object. A party tabling a proposal may thus wish to create the appearance of general agreement to dissuade potential naysayers.
- During the negotiation process, a negotiator should stop at intervals to review her actions to ensure she is on track to securing her top priorities. The Negotiator's Pause[2] can be both a "scheduled" pause, as well as one that a negotiator learns to use in the heat of the moment to regain control of herself.
- To avoid misinterpretation, it is important that a negotiator's messages are clear. Every statement sends a signal, so speak with intention and be vague only if you intend to do so.
- In tense moments, emotions can run high and a negotiator may exhibit "legacy" behaviors, so-called because her behavior is not easily forgotten, even if it is "out of character" for her. Legacy behaviors affect a negotiator's reputation and credibility. For a negotiator, managing her reputation is critical.
- Verify that the language of a negotiated outcome promotes feasible action that all parties are committed to implementing. There is not much point in agreeing to something on paper if no one can, or is going to, do anything about it.

Aren't interests and positions the same thing? (Chapter 2)

- Familiarity with your counterparts' interests, especially which set of interests tends to dominate in which situations, can help you see through their bargaining positions – the narrative and strategy they use to achieve their interests. Getting past this bargaining position is key to finding solutions that meets some of your counterpart's priorities.
- To understand a person's interests, one must first get their perspective. One of the most effective ways is through the "ladder of inference" model.[3] This approach focuses on the use of advocacy and inquiry when two or more people are communicating, while helping each party understand the realities the other is working with. It is important to take our counterparts down their "ladder of inference" through inquiry, before we take them up our own. Trust and empathy are key foundations for employing the "ladder of inference," as our counterparts may be reluctant to explain the data, interpretations and assumptions used to support their conclusions unless we have displayed we can be trusted to patiently empathize with (without necessarily agreeing to) their perspectives. By understanding the significance and focus our counterparts place on their experiences and the information they have, we can better explain why we have made different assumptions and interpretations from the available data. This can put us in

a better position to persuade them to draw a different conclusion from before.

- A negotiator needs to be self-aware and attentive to her distractions, biases, and overall mindset when preparing for and taking part in a negotiation. Self-awareness is key so that a negotiator knows her own set of interests, particularly which is dominating, so she can decide whether to "rein in" a particular interest or whether another set should come out more strongly.

The insider's guide to the UN negotiation system (Chapter 3)

- Negotiators can better understand the system in which their negotiation is taking place by identifying (i) the key personalities involved in the negotiation; (ii) the timeline for decision-making; and (iii) the negotiation's history.
- As part of understanding the negotiation's history, a negotiator should familiarize herself with (i) historical concepts and phrases used in the negotiation – precedence; (ii) code words, which may be used to obscure or to clarify; and (iii) the workload of fellow negotiators so that approaches can be better strategized. A negotiation's history can also provide tips on resolving disagreements.
- To resolve language disagreements in a UN negotiation, negotiators often resort to three tactics: (i) using "agreed language," which is phrases from resolutions previously adopted by the UN; (ii) "cancelling out" conflicting proposals by deleting all proposals on the issue; and (iii) using vague language. These tactics should be used judiciously, so as not to perpetuate agreements that have little additional value.

Don't go it alone: building relationships and alliances (Chapter 4)

- Regardless of a proposal's merit, UN delegations may resist it merely because of its proponent. If the negotiator putting forward the proposal is unknown, disliked, or not respected, or if the proposal comes from the "wrong" delegation, the proposal is probably dead in the water. In general, any truly original proposal at the UN – especially from a "new" negotiator – is guilty of "interference" until proven innocent.
- The ability of a negotiator to effectively achieve her goals through creativity and compromise greatly depends on her rapport with others. If the rapport is good, she is more likely to get help when in a bind or receive some latitude when she has to promote an unpopular position.
- There are a variety of UN delegates a negotiator will encounter and therefore a variety of relationships that she should cultivate. At the risk of overgeneralising, we have categorised the most essential: *friendlies* (delegations with similar views); *opposites* (delegations with differing views); *key personalities* (which include *power players, problem solvers, and spoilers*); and *quiets and neutrals* (often, the majority). The categories are not mutually

exclusive, though rapport with each benefits from a specialized approach to relationship building. The most successful negotiators attempt to build relationships with everyone.

- To overcome prejudice when tabling a proposal, a proponent has several options in the form of alliances (none of which are mutually exclusive), including (i) introducing the idea as a group proposal through a formal alliance, be it from an existing group or a new alliance forged to promote that particular initiative; (ii) having a more "accepted" delegation present (or front) the proposal via a temporary alliance; and (iii) lobbying respected negotiators from other delegations who will speak up for the proposal, thereby forming a flexible alliance.
- We recommend building a networking plan for each negotiation, based on the positions you need to promote or defend. Use your own attributes to their best advantage, approaching networking as an integral part of your job.
- Groups are a powerful, and in some cases permanent, form of alliance. They can augment a member delegation's influence and authority exponentially; they can also cause additional headaches, for both group members and those negotiating with them.

Welcome to Negotiations Theater: an off-Broadway production (Chapter 5)

- Official negotiations are useful for parties to deliver messages to their various audiences, but can be limiting in their public nature. Informal negotiations provide a safe space for negotiators to have difficult conversations, brainstorm options, and piece together a final deal, all without being "tied" to public statements. In any negotiation, it is important to establish and organize the time and space (both formal and informal) for delegates to come together as individuals working toward a shared result.
- In negotiations that involve multiple parties, the key players may come together informally to make difficult and complex tradeoffs aimed at cutting a final deal. Fewer players at the table translates into fewer conflicting interests, but risks alienating those not involved, potentially endangering the deal. Despite the additional noise, it is useful to be more inclusive, as people like to be a part of the solution. If the stakes in a negotiation are important to a delegation, its negotiator needs to be a part of these informal conversations.
- Once an outcome is achieved within a small group, it is important to socialize it more broadly. This involves reaching out to key players and having a (or several) convincing narrative(s). When conducting outreach, it is important to tailor the narrative to the stakeholder while maintaining a genuine and consistent narrative that reinforces your credibility as an interlocutor.

- Although much of the work essential to a good compromise takes place behind the scenes, the dynamics at the formal negotiation table have the potential to make or break a carefully crafted outcome. Both formal and informal processes have essential – and reciprocal – roles to play in negotiations.
- When difficult conversations need to happen in the public space in negotiations, theater can ensue. For an experienced negotiator, the use of theater is a strategic move, calculated to get to the best outcome. Delegates also employ theater to act out a final compromise in the public space, demonstrating to the "audience" the legitimacy of an outcome negotiated behind the scenes. There are different manifestations of negotiation theater, some constructive and some destructive, all of which are prevalent in the UN context.
- Negotiating with capital is an important component of a UN delegate's job. It is in her interest to cultivate a good relationship with her "desk," building trust, offering context, providing updates, and building arguments to support the final agreement.

I call this meeting to order: chairing UN negotiations (Chapter 6)

- Chairs at the UN are usually appointed in a personal capacity; i.e. a Chair is the individual, not the country. This concept of "personal capacity" is important to the legitimacy of a multilateral process, although there are exceptions to the "personal capacity" rule for certain UN conferences. Likewise, the Chair should not confuse a country's position in a UN negotiation with the individual representing it.
- At the UN, the Chair needs to understand the big picture, but not necessarily be an expert on the subjects being negotiated (although this helps!). Instead, she needs to be an expert on the process.
- As highlighted by Ambassador Tommy Koh,[4] a successful Chair exhibits specific behaviors and qualities, including being humble, respectful, fair, transparent, trustworthy, a good listener, proactive, calm, courageous, a good mediator and bridge builder, and inspiring, among others. Ambassador Koh also recommends nine approaches for a successful Chairpersonship: (i) master your brief; (ii) use your bureau; (iii) work with the secretariat; (iv) be a team player and team builder; (v) avoid setting up secret negotiating groups; (vi) create an inclusive, transparent and orderly negotiation process; (vii) respect the importance of timing; (viii) actively garner support and seek to accommodate; and (ix) work well with the NGOs.
- In steering the negotiation process forward, the Chair needs to track all the players and their evolving positions. At times, the Chair needs to be a mediator; at others, she becomes an admonishing parent; at other critical moments, she is an encouraging cheerleader, allowing the parties to resolve issues by themselves. However, helping parties reach a sustainable outcome does not always mean a document adopted by consensus at the UN.

- Three common mistakes a Chair should avoid: (i) attempting to achieve an outcome agreed by consensus, even if the consensus is not there; (ii) becoming drunk with power; and (iii) falling victim to a negotiation gone awry.

Mitigating asymmetric power: the 800-pound gorilla and the fearless ant (Chapter 7)

- Large UN Member States can demand a lead role in multilateral negotiations; at times, others de facto yield these countries or large groups that role. Although an enlightened use of such power can produce positive outcomes, the imbalance also has the potential to negatively affect the tone of a negotiation, as well as undermine the perceived legitimacy of an eventual agreement.
- Larger delegations should not seek to take over a negotiation. Likewise, smaller countries should not defer to larger countries, assuming they will take the lead. With the opportunity to have a voice on the world stage comes a responsibility to act, regardless of size.
- Smaller countries – and their individual delegates – have some distinct advantages over larger countries and their representatives. To seize the opportunity inherent in being an "ant," and to have greater impact on any negotiation, try (i) acting as a bridge; (ii) forming alliances; (iii) taking on a leadership role in the negotiation process; (iv) speaking up; and (v) thinking outside the script.
- Delegates from "gorilla" countries need to develop an awareness of the potential impact of their relative power on the dynamics of the process and the efficacy of an agreement. These delegates can counteract the negative effects by adopting a number of behaviors, including (i) displaying a willingness to find mutual solutions; (ii) actively cooperating; (iii) responsively listening; (iv) being respectful; (v) not hogging the floor; and (vi) choosing their battles.

I am a female negotiator: so what? (Chapter 8)

- Stories shared by our female colleagues demonstrate the complex challenges faced by female negotiators at the UN. Although attitudes and behavioral differences are certainly accentuated by cultural norms and individual characteristics, there remain common elements that make a woman's experience in UN negotiations different from that of a man.
- Individuals taking part in a negotiation play a large part in dictating the negotiation process and outcome. The individual in the room matters, as do the dynamics between those assembled. A negotiator should do her best to adapt to any culturally-dictated, socially-inept, or gender-inappropriate attitudes diplomatically and without losing a sense of what she represents and what her delegation is hoping to accomplish; there is always a difficult

actor or circumstance, and an experienced negotiator – male or female – rolls with the punches, to the extent reasonable. At the same time, female negotiators are rightly calling for equal treatment, challenging stereotypes and behaviors that are no longer acceptable in the workplace.

Please excuse us as we upgrade our process ... and software (Chapter 9)

- To improve the UN negotiation process, delegations can consider: (i) reducing the number of resolutions tabled each year and bringing more focus to each resolution; (ii) encouraging a culture of innovation; and (iii) providing more training for negotiators.
- Many interactions and processes at the UN benefit from the use of digital technology; there are also areas where traditional tools of negotiation still hold value, and still others where technology has had unintended consequences. Face-to-face negotiations are important in themselves, and ultimately irreplaceable for building long-term trust and humanizing counterparts.

Concluding thoughts

Although negotiation skills can be taught, negotiating is also an art, unique to each person. The presence of each individual negotiator has a significant impact, as each person shapes the negotiation process and the negotiated outcome differently. So the key question is really: what kind of UN negotiator will *that* person be?

Hence, our vision of passing on our knowledge and experience to help frame how negotiators view their craft and to empower the next generation to speak for a better world. This book contains concepts into which we wish we had had more insight as we began our UN tours. Chief among these is that the person – the individual negotiator – has both power and responsibility; how they wield them matters.

In the examples we have included throughout the book, this clear theme emerges: the individual negotiator matters as much, and sometimes more than, the flag in a UN negotiation. How each delegate conducts herself in the negotiation, how she approaches a problem and interacts with colleagues, often dictates the outcome even more than country positions do. At the UN, there are times that call for tough tactics; however, so much can be accomplished, including building (and re-building) bridges on the world stage, through basic humanity – respect, listening, patience, empathy, and kindness.

Former UN Secretary-General Dag Hammarskjöld recognized that while the UN is not a perfect world organization, it is a young experiment in the history of humanity.[5] To us, this means the UN is not fixed in stone, so while we have to be careful not to weaken it, we also have the opportunity *and the responsibility* to shape and improve it. The three of us fell in love with the UN because we see the eminent possibilities of using this framework to its fullest capacity –

not only to prevent war but to pursue sustainable living in a peaceful world. We hope this book inspires you to learn more about the UN and to use your personal power to speak for the world.

Notes

1 Craig Lambert, "The Psyche on Automatic," *Harvard Magazine*, November-December 2010 (2010), http://harvardmagazine.com/2010/11/the-psyche-on-automatic.
2 Adapted by CMPartners, LLC. Used with permission, 2018.
3 This adaptation of the Ladder of Inference (C. Argyris) is used with permission of CMPartners LLC, 2018.
4 Tommy Koh, "The art of chairing conferences: lessons learnt," in *The Tommy Koh Reader: Favourite Essays and Lectures* (Singapore: World Scientific, 2013), 238–244.
5 Kai Falkman, *To Speak for the World: Speeches and Statements by Dag Hammarskjold* (Stockholm: Atlantis, 2005).

References

Coppola, Francis Ford, dir. The Godfather. 1972; Hollywood, CA: Paramount Pictures and Alfran Productions, 2001. DVD.

Donoghue, David, Felix Dodds and Jimena Leiva Roesch, *Negotiating the Sustainable Development Goals: A Transformational Agenda in an Insecure World*. London: Taylor & Francis Group, 2016.

Erickson, Amanda. "What 'Personal Space' Looks Like Around the World." *The Washington Post*, 24 April 2017.

Eyal, Tal, Nicholas Epley, and Mary Steffel. "Perspective Mistaking: Accurately Understanding the Mind of Another Requires Getting Perspective, Not Taking Perspective." *Journal of Personality and Social Psychology*. Vol. 114, No. 4, (2018): 547–571.

Falkman, Kai. *To Speak for the World: Speeches and Statements by Dag Hammarskjöld, Secretary-General of the United Nations 1953–1961*. Stockholm: Atlantis, 2005.

Fasulo, Linda M. *An Insider's Guide to the UN*. New Haven: Yale University Press, 2004.

Fisher, Roger, Ury William, and Bruce Patton. *Getting to Yes: Negotiating Agreement without Giving In*, 2nd ed. New York, N.Y.: Penguin Books, 1991.

Griffiths, Martin. *The Prisoner of Peace: An interview with Kofi A. Annan*. Centre for Humanitarian Dialogue (2008). https://reliefweb.int/sites/reliefweb.int/files/resources/6F9DC0AD3921DFA7C12575890033E862-Full_Report.pdf

Koh, Tommy. "My Experiences with the WTO Dispute Settlement System." In *Economic Diplomacy*, edited by Margaret Liang and C.L. Lim. Singapore: World Scientific, 2011.

Koh, Tommy. "The art of chairing conferences: lessons learnt." In *The Tommy Koh Reader: Favourite Essays and Lectures*. Singapore: World Scientific, 2013.

Lambert, Craig. "The Psyche on Automatic." *Harvard Magazine*. November-December (2010). http://harvardmagazine.com/2010/11/the-psyche-on-automatic.

Liang, Margaret. "Anti-Dumping Negotiations in the Uruguay Round." In *Economic Diplomacy*, edited by Margaret Liang and C.L. Lim. Singapore: World Scientific Publishing Co Pte Ltd, 2011.

Livni, Ephrat. "There's Only One Way to Truly Understand Another Person's Mind." *Quartz*, 3 July 2018.

Macharia, Kamau, Pamela Chasek and David O'Connor. *Transforming Multilateral Diplomacy*. London: Taylor & Francis Group, 2018.

Miller, Claire Cain. "Women Actually do Govern Differently." *The New York Times*, 10 November 2016.

Power, Samantha. "Samantha Power: My friend, the Russian Ambassador." *The New York Times*, 25 February 2017.

Sandberg, Sheryl. *Lean In: Women, Work, and the Will to Lead*. New York: Alfred A. Knopf, 2013.

Stone, Douglas, Bruce Patton, and Sheila Heen. *Difficult Conversations: How to Discuss What Matters Most*, Kindle edition. New York: Penguin, 2011.

Tiwari, Sivakant. "Intellectual Property Rights in the Uruguay Round." In *Economic Diplomacy*, edited by Margaret Liang and C.L. Lim. Singapore: World Scientific, 2011.

United Nations. *Charter of the United Nations*. 24 October 1945.

United Nations. *Basic Facts about the United Nations 42nd Edition*. New York: UN, 2017.

United Nations Department of Information. "The United Nations System." Last modified March 13, 2017. Accessed May 23, 2018. http://www.un.org/en/aboutun/structure/pdfs/UN%20System%20Chart_ENG_FINAL_MARCH13_2017.pdf

UN News. "Feature: A conversation with female ambassadors about the UN Security Council." *UN News*. 17 March 2016. https://news.un.org/en/story/2016/03/524642-feature-conversation-female-ambassadors-about-un-security-council

Zartman, I. William. "The Timing of Peace Initiatives: Hurting Stalemates and Ripe Moments." *The Global Review of Ethnopolitics*. Vol. *1*, no. 1(2001): 8–18.

Index

Page numbers appearing in italics refer to figures.

Made in United States
North Haven, CT
28 January 2025

65078037R00098